I'M NOT DONE YET!

A Memoir

COBBY M. WILLIAMS

C. Mondale Publishing

I'm Not Done Yet
Cobby M. Williams

Published by C.Mondale Publishing
1853 Ontario Pl, NW
Washington, DC 20009

ISBN: 979-8-218-65240-1 (Paperback)

To learn more about the author or contact for speaking engagements, go to:
www.cobbymwilliams.com or imwithcobby@gmail.com

For permission requests, write to the publisher, addressed "Attention: Permissions Coordinator," at the email addresses:
Imwithcobby@gmail.com / Imwithcore@gmail.com

TABLE OF CONTENTS

Dedication 5

Chapter 1: The Moment My Life Changed 7

Chapter 2: My Village 15

Chapter 3: Working Day and Night 30

Chapter 4: College Boy 46

Chapter 5: Culture Shock 64

Chapter 6: A New Journey 77

Chapter 7: Fighting Vicious Words and Making 92
          History

Chapter 8: Not Bouncing Back 103

Chapter 9: The Best of Both Worlds 116

Chapter 10: Another New Beginning 127

Chapter 11: The Longest Year of My Life 140

DEDICATION

To the following people, I dedicate this book:

To my mom.

To my father who died when I was just six years old.

To my family, friends, and supporters who helped me along this journey.

To little boys and girls who grew up sharing and having to accept "hand me downs."

To teens who are living from house to house, family to family.

To teens who had to fight over food during breakfast, lunch, or dinner with their siblings.

To college students, who suffered through college not knowing where the next dollar would come from.

To kids of single mothers and fathers who are raising themselves and their siblings while your parent(s) is working multiple jobs.

To adults who don't believe in themselves and feel like giving up when no one else believes in you.

A gem is not polished without rubbing, nor a man perfected without trials.

— Chinese Proverb

CHAPTER 1

THE MOMENT MY LIFE CHANGED

Unspoken words swirled inside my head as Mom's voice droned on in the background. For the life of me I can't seem to remember what we were arguing about, but I can still hear the aggravation in her voice as she made her frustrations known in a way only a mother could. She didn't speak much unless you made her mad. She had a soft voice that turned into a shrill, high pitch when she was angry.

That afternoon, I had clearly gone too far because her voice was shrill like she had sucked in helium from a balloon. I had a lot of important questions for my mother, but she was rarely home so I had to get answers whenever I could. Apparently, that day, she wasn't in the mood for being the Wizard of Oz, but I was annoyed and couldn't wait any longer for answers.

"I don't give a damn!" I bellowed at my mother and, in my mind, our argument had come to an end. I started walking toward the front door. Mom shouted back, but her words went in one ear and out of the other. I laced my sneakers and shook my head, not responding to my mother while my younger brother, Raymond, stood in the shadows.

Raymond's 14-year-old, disappointed face grew into

a scowl, "You hear Mama talking to you?" He called himself checking me, questioning me in an unforgiving, but naïve tone.

Ignoring him, I called out to my oldest brother, Jeremy, whom we called JJ, and snatched open the heavy, front door as his footsteps descended the stairs in a heated rush. I could tell Raymond didn't understand my anger as he watched in disbelief while we prepared to leave the house. I was still ignoring Mom's demands as they pierced every corner of the first floor of our home.

We lived in a nice, 4-bedroom, 2-bathroom, blue house on East Mays Street in Jackson, Mississippi, in 1993. There was no screen door, so the slam of the wooden front door against the door frame was deafening. The moment we opened the door, the humidity of Mississippi was damn near stifling. *Why is Mississippi so hot?* I wondered silently.

"Whew, it's hot," JJ said exactly what I was thinking, as we shuffled past my eight-year-old sister, Kennedy, and her friends who were playing outside in the yard. He was thinking the same thing as me and, without saying another word, I wiped the beads of perspiration from my forehead and JJ waved to a chick from across the street, as I kept my focus on the sidewalk ahead. We took off sprinting down the street toward the basketball courts. Both JJ and I loved basketball, so the court seemed to be the best place to clear our heads of the major blowup that had just happened back at home.

As usual, the streets of Jackson were already bustling with people on every corner. JT, a small-time dealer, stood on the corner selling his product in the open. Fiends approached him to receive their daily dose of poison without a care in the world. That's how some folks in Jackson rolled. When he saw JJ and I walk by, he nodded his head in acknowledgment, and I nodded back in response.

JJ turned his attention away from JT's enterprise, noticing my no-nonsense attitude, and asked, "What did you do to make Mama mad?" He tried to hide a chuckle. JJ was four years older than me and sometimes, when it came to the things I did, all he could do was laugh.

More often than not we found ourselves getting on our mother's last nerve. It was funny because it seemed like every nerve, we hit was the last one, but the next day, sure enough, we'd hit the last one again, which is understandable when you consider a woman trying to raise three boys, practically alone. At that time, I was in my last stage of puberty, and things were getting uncomfortable for both of us. So often me and Mom bumped heads as I was trying to understand things she wasn't ready for me to understand.

I shook my head at JJ. I was not in the mood to discuss anything other than a game of "pick-up." As we approached Calloway High School, a roaring mixture of voices enveloped us before we even reached the black-topped domain where the two full-length basketball courts were jam packed. No matter what time of day or night, the courts remained packed with people. This was the hangout spot for fellas who wanted to show off their skills, or take their frustrations out on the court, and the girls who loved to watch them and cheer them on. The heightened emotions of competitive sports combined with raging hormones was a dangerous mixture, but we loved the excitement of being in that atmosphere.

JJ and I walked to the edge of the basketball court near the bleachers, where everyone seemed to congregate. I dapped up a few of my friends and greeted several people I knew from around the way. Most were guys I'd met in high school and others who relocated to Jackson from other parts of Mississippi, like me.

At that time, I was sixteen and we lived in a predominately Black, middle-class neighborhood where people were primarily judged by a few details. The unspoken burden was always about accurately representing the parts of Jackson you hailed from. You could tell where they were from by the conversations people were having, the clothes and colors they wore and the gang affiliations they had. There was a lot we could decode about a person even based on the designer labels they wore.

It seemed like everyone had their own unique way of proving they were "the man" on the basketball court. This day was no different. Fellas on the court brought out their best moves and worst attitudes during routine pick-up games. We watched as the games grew progressively intense. Two guys started arguing and cussing at each other. Their friends noticed the uproar and broke up the fight before things got too crazy. Unmoved by the chaos, my friends continued talking as if nothing happened.

Once the friends of the guys fighting finally separated them, the dueling pair left the basketball court. Assured the drama was over, the game resumed. Now, I was on the court. JJ sat on the sidelines, but shortly after he sat down, he was no longer watching me. He affixed his gaze on a guy briskly walking towards us onto the court.

Without warning, the sound of gunfire pierced through the scorching heat, sounding off behind me. My senses immediately sharpened and my adrenaline started racing. I turned around to run but I felt a searing pain in my thigh. I hollered out in agony and collapsed to the ground. I could hear people screaming, crying, and yelling in the distance as people scattered in all directions. All I saw was the back of my teammates' heads as they fled the scene.

Suddenly, I felt alone. Laying on the ground, frozen in pain and fear, I heard my grandmother's voice saying, "Be still, Cobby." Then, somehow, I felt calm amid the chaos.

Everyone dispersed except JJ. It seemed to me, as his younger brother, that there was nothing he was afraid of. I watched him run towards me, not taking his eyes off the gunman, who stood over me, with a black and white bandanna covering his nose and mouth. The gunman's eyes narrowed as he looked me in the eye and pulled back the hammer. I stared at him in frightened shock. With my widened eyes, I could see the rage in his eyes and realized that this man, whoever he was, wanted to kill me.

I guess it's true what they say, when you think you're about to die, everything moves in slow motion. We glared at each other. He steadied his hand and aimed the barrel right between my eyes. I stared at that weapon in his clutch as the brief life I'd lived, literally, flashed before me. My thoughts, previously clouded by anger, suddenly became clear.

I was a sixteen year old junior at Murrah High School. Sixteen is supposed to be one of the best years of every young man's life. However, when I thought about my childhood, my siblings, and the unfortunate last words I spoke to my mother, I regretted, more than anything, yelling at her earlier that day.

My mother was beautiful. She had dimples like me, that sunk deep into her hazelnut skin. When she smiled, her high cheek bones made her squint. Her long, black hair shook back and forth across the back of her hospital scrubs as we stood, arguing, in the living room.

I'm sorry, Mama, were the words I wish I could have said to her. Now, at that moment, I still couldn't muster any words with a gun in my face and blood gushing from my thigh. I was in a fixated stare. I didn't blink.

Then, the shooter had a thought more gruesome than killing me.

He looked at JJ and aimed the gun at him. Words lodged in my throat as I helplessly watched him pull the trigger. *Not, JJ's life for mine*, is what I wanted to say, but I couldn't. The gun clicked and then silence. It jammed and the gunman retreated as swiftly as he had approached, wielding the weapon at anyone in his path to his getaway car.

My brother kneeled down beside me and applied pressure to my gushing wound. Blood was pouring out from my leg like a broken fire hydrant. For a moment, I lost all sense of fear. Someone called the ambulance and the EMTs loaded me onto a gurney and into the back of the emergency vehicle. JJ rode with me. "We're going to cut these shorts," the lady said. She followed the bullet trail to where it had ended. In my vanity, I couldn't help thinking, *Today would be the day I wore these... boxers from now on!* "Had it been just a couple of more inches," the EMT continued in a serious tone, "You wouldn't be here with us."

The desire I harbored for revenge was like a rat gnawing at my soul, relentless and unceasing. I spent days in the hospital replaying the events from that day on the court. *What if my brother had been shot in the head?* If JJ had died, that would have crushed me. I knew he was afraid, too, but he remained close, comforting me. It brought us closer together, despite our differences and attitudes towards each other.

As I lay in that hospital bed, I realized how close to death I was. The bullet had pierced through my thigh, stopping two inches shy of my scrotum. When I understood more of what the doctors were saying about the seriousness of my gunshot wound, the sudden realization of my circumstances hit me like a Mack truck.

After spending three days in the hospital, I had murder on my mind. Every time I flinched from the pain, the anger within me grew more ferocious, festering like a septic wound, and the only effective antibiotic was cold, hard revenge, thoughts a sixteen-year-old should never possess. It was the most emotionally intense moment in my life.

The police and local news reported the incident as a gang-related shooting. I wasn't in a gang, but I was associated closely enough to one. I was the textbook definition of "guilty by association," although I never learned why I was shot or who did it.

The shooting wasn't an abnormal occurrence for the area around the basketball courts in the park by the Calloway High School. People were always scared for their safety in Jackson, but the activity around the courts slowed down for a few weeks after I was shot. In my heart, I knew God saved me and my brother that day, but I couldn't wrap my head around why.

CHAPTER 2

MY VILLAGE

The last time I heard gunshots that close to me was at my father's funeral. It was loud and, since I was only six years old at the time it, startled me. As unsettling as it was, the deafening blasts into the air were the sound of honor and respect for a soldier who had nobly done his duty. I never imagined in my wildest dreams, that I'd hear those same sounds and feeling the thunderous impact of a bullet piercing through my body just ten years later. This gunshot had nothing to do with honor or respect. This gunshot could have been the end of my life.

While I laid in the hospital with my thoughts swirling in my head, I didn't just think about my mother and brother, I thought about the rest of my family, too. *What would have happened in their lives if I had died then?* I shuddered at the thought of leaving them here to pick up the pieces without me. Some people become family through birth. Others become a part of your tribe through marriage and after I left the hospital I learned, there are some family members that you choose yourself.

JJ's father found his way back into my mom's life after my father passed away. I referred to him as my stepfather when talking to others, but the truth is, I never even knew if he and my mother got married. I don't remember an engagement party, a wedding, or even a reception. In any case, my mother loved that man. No matter what he did, he always seemed to find a way back into her good graces and our home. Don't get me wrong, there were many good qualities about my stepfather and we had some good moments, yet there were days and nights that I'd rather forget because of him.

On the positive side, he taught me how to stay focused, how to keep the main thing the main thing. He used to either walk with me or drive me to school in the mornings. On our walks I often found myself distracted by the grown men shooting dice or playing card games on the side of buildings. I noticed no matter what the game, there was always money present.

I was the curious kid amongst my siblings. Every time I stopped to observe how the men on the street corners played the dice game, my brothers would yell, "Come on, let's go!" The guys on the corner found my innocent curiosity hilarious, but my stepfather didn't find it funny at all. I'll never forget the day I received my first lesson in rolling dice. We were heading toward school and one of the known street hustlers handed me the dice and asked me to roll. The older gentleman placed the dice in my hand and laid out the rules of the game.

"If you roll this number, I win," he said. "If you roll this number, I break—"

Before he could speak the last word, my stepfather yelled out of the car window, "Get your ass to school, boy!" I didn't get to roll the dice...that day.

It seemed like the only time I could remember when my stepfather wasn't yelling was during holidays. It was during Christmas that I witnessed how a man's temperament could set the tone for his entire household. When my stepfather was in a good mood, we all felt safe, secure, and loved. The problem was that I knew every year the holiday season would come to an end and my stepfather would be returning to his more normal, but unpleasant, disposition.

As children, we look to our parents for an example of how to behave and how to mature. Sometimes our parents turn out to be examples of what not to do. My stepfather was an angry man who, instead of dealing with his anger, took his emotions out on his family. Everyone in my household bore the brunt of many unnecessary beatings and we lived in constant fear of his constant emotional instability.

My stepfather's mood depended upon the amount of liquor in his system. He fluctuated between a raging bull and a placated version of him that seethed with anger just below the surface. I know my stepfather loved my siblings and I by how he treated us when he wasn't drunk or in a financial bind. It's just that I don't remember those loving times as often as I have nightmares about the crying, arguing, fighting and beatings.

Our living situation was a result of the constant instability. We moved around from place to place, between

Canton and Jackson, like nomads. Every time Mom enrolled us in a different school, we were withdrawn a few months later, just as abruptly as we had enrolled. I suppose it was our nomadic lifestyle helped foster my love for traveling and being comfortable adapting to unfamiliar environments. Still, we moved so much, sometimes I felt homeless. I was always thinking, *"Damn, we're gonna move again because of one man. I have to get out of this situation!"* I certainly had to learn how to bounce back from so many experiences, seemingly unscathed. I simply wanted out of the situation quite honestly. As a young man, it's hard to imagine the possibility of bouncing back from so many challenges when you've barely had a chance to stand still.

My parents' volatile relationship teetered on the line between love and hate, leaving deep scars on my troubled heart. There were endless, loud arguments and physical fights. My mom was hospitalized more times than I want to remember. There was one night, though, that I'll never forget.

I recall my stepfather coming home late at night and piss drunk. He wanted Mom to give him money and she refused, so he started a fight. I was asleep and heard the argument, but I was in this strange sleep mode where I wanted to wake up, but I couldn't. Have you ever felt frozen in your sleep and unable to open your eyes? That was me. I imagine this is what sleep paralysis feels like.

When I could finally shake the sleep off and wake up, I ran to the kitchen to find the biggest knife we had. It wasn't there. The next thing I saw was my stepfather, butt-naked, beating my mother. *Where is JJ?* I don't know why he wasn't home. He wouldn't have let this happen to Mom. The only thing I could think to do is run next door to our Chinese neighbor's home. He came over and helped my mom.

When my neighbor called 911, my stepfather left the house. The police arrived and an ambulance came and took my mother's beaten-up body to the hospital. I didn't go back to sleep. I spent the rest of the night crying uncontrollably.

I wanted to kill that man and bury him under an unpainted rock. I'm not saying that my mom was a saint, but it hurt me to not be able to stand up for her. I was just too little and young to speak up. The sight of him made me feel like a vicious dog that was foaming at the mouth and being held back by his owner. I made up my mind that no one would ever beat me up like that. Little did I know I was about to spend a lot of my teen years getting into fights, but it became known that I was not going to take defeat easily. They just didn't know why I felt like I had nothing to lose. One person who had to learn that was a bully named FeFe.

FeFe was rather tall, with wide shoulders and a pudgy stomach. He kicked my ass two to three times per week. After being knocked down several times, I gained the strength to fight back. FeFe's relentless attacks taught me how to stand up for myself and fight back, even with the odds stacked against me. It was either take the beating or get better at fighting back. Fighting FeFe helped me get better when I had to fight others.

FeFe had an older brother named Marcus. After multiple confrontations with FeFe, I joined alliances with Marcus and his older brother. That decision changed everything. When FeFe saw Marcus and I talking, he would look the other way. The same level of fear I felt about FeFe he felt from Mike and Marcus. So, the attacks from FeFe stopped.

To this day, I still have nightmares about the traumatic events that occurred within our home in Canton. It was the home that Mom purchased using the proceeds from my late father's life insurance policy. This was also the first of many homes we absconded from in fear.

On my last day of school in Canton, via the intercom, the secretary summoned me to the primary office, where I walked in considerable trepidation. The moment I walked into the office and laid eyes on my cousin, I felt my life would change forever, I just didn't know how. Sadly, I was correct in my assumption. We never returned to that three-bedroom home near Fred's Dollar Store again.

After we moved from Canton, our family settled in the Briarwood Apartments of Jackson, Mississippi, which was the beginning of us moving from one address after another. During the seemlingly long drive down the highway to Jackson, as questions I was too young and naïve to ask clouded my mind. *Was my family in trouble?*

So much of my childhood seemed to be looking for a way to escape. Sports were my escape. My stepfather built us a basketball goal in the backyard. It was a hand-made wooden backboard hoisted up on a long wooden pole, and an iron rim. Neighbors and friends from all across the town would come to play on the dirty ground and sometimes muddy soil. We played flag football and basketball in our backyard with the kids in the neighborhood. Basketball and football were the universal way to meet and connect with them. Sports kept our minds off the toils of life...temporarily.

Though I didn't spend much time with my friends in Canton, once we moved, I didn't forget any of them... nor did I forget any of my enemies. We all shared a bond through basketball or football. We were Cantonians. They were my village. All that ended, though, when we disappeared to Jackson.

Eventually, I learned how to communicate my emotions with my words instead of my hands. If I could be grateful for anything, I thank my stepfather for showing me what not to do, but also giving me access to other family members who I developed strong bonds with. Through my stepfather's relationship with Mom, I had the benefit of extended family members who looked after me when I couldn't take care of myself. I didn't know much about my biological father's parents at the time because they lived in Kansas City, Missouri, but between Mom's and my stepfather's family, relatives were always close — less than a mile or within walking distance. My favorite nearby relative was Aunt Stein.

Aunt Stein was the sister of my stepfather's mother. Aunt Stein meant the world to me! She was a nurturer, who comforted me whenever I was in her presence. When I came to visit or stayed the night, she brushed my hair constantly. It's the reason my hair is wavy and curly 'til this day and I still get a lot of haircuts! She always had my favorite cereal, Kellogg's Frosted Flakes®. It does have the taste adults have grown to love! Most importantly, Aunt Stein taught me about the Bible in a way that I could fully understand. She would make sure we prayed "The Evening Prayer":

Now, I lay me down to sleep
I pray my Lord my soul to keep
If I should die before I wake
I pray, my Lord, my soul to take.

Even though it was kind of frightening to think about dying in my sleep, somehow the way she said these words brought me comfort. The kind of comfort that could make a troubled soul sleep peacefully knowing that someone, something out there was covering my innocence and giving much needed rest from the stress that didn't belong to a little boy.

Aunt Stein had four working teenagers of her own. They treated me like a little brother. Her middle child, Timothy, was one of my mentors growing up. Timothy was fair skinned with green eyes and a total girl magnet. I must admit, I kind of admired him for that. He took me under his wing and protected me. No one messed with me when he was around. I spent my childhood defending myself and helping my family survive just below the poverty line, which has kept me in fight-or-flight mode my entire life. But Timothy was a blessing to me.

I had to walk through multiple neighborhoods to get to Aunt Stein's house. These were middle-class, Black neighborhoods. Each time I visited, I wondered what those families did for a living, with nice cars parked outside their homes. The neighborhoods were quaint and quiet, with gated lawns, which was night and day from the corner store just a few blocks away. During the summer, the store owners offered me hot dogs or hamburgers off their grills. Timothy would always show up to walk me the rest of the way to his house. I needed people like Aunt Stein and Timothy in my life because some nights at home were just too traumatic and unsafe. We needed other places to go and Aunt Stein's was one of those safe places.

Another safe place was my grandmother's house. My grandmother was a professional and watching her work inspired me and made me realize that not everyone had to work in blue-collar positions to survive. She was slim, fair-skinned, and only five feet tall. Visiting Grandma's house was always exciting.

She was an insurance broker, and her home served a dual purpose as an office. She served people from all levels of society. Some dressed in business suits and left their shoes at the front door before entering her home, which was customary back then, as they handled their business in her living room. A tough businesswoman who I admired, Grandma was a fantastic cook who always had dinner or dessert waiting on the stove upon arrival. That was her way of showing love and I loved to receive her love! "Oh, Cobby, Cobby, Cobby!" she would say all the time.

On our way to her house, I used to stop by the corner store, Wen and Cheeks, to pick up my favorite snack (glazed donuts). The store sat amongst a series of businesses like laundromats, barbershops, and hair salons. It was such a high traffic area; you never knew the people you would encounter throughout the day. No matter the time of day, there would be people smoking weed, drinking forty-ounce beers, or some kind of white or brown liquor. They self-medicated and passed the day away like there were no worries in the world. This was where I received my street education. If I didn't hear it at home, I heard it from the corner. I learned my first curse words, witnessed multiple street transactions, and plenty of fights.

Growing up in Canton toughened me up. The area

was like the movie, 300. We kept our army close and defended the Cantonians with fierce loyalty. You had to face every obstacle and push through it, or else. I saw women and men fighting and families feuding with other families over owing money to each other. Canton was my first home of many, after moving from Kansas City, Missouri, at two years old. Shoved into small pockets of the city, the slight concentration of the Black community lacked opportunities and an absence of higher education aspirations created an environment infertile for economic success. This didn't sit well with me and when I discovered it, I wanted to do something about it, but I had my own problems to deal with first.

I don't know why, but I repeated the second grade at McNeal Elementary School in Canton. Perhaps I had too many distractions at home. Perhaps I just couldn't focus enough to demonstrate what I'd learned. In any case, other students teased me relentlessly. I vowed to never repeat another grade or have anyone refer to me as a dummy or a kid with a deficiency. My stepfather and some of his family treated Raymond and I like outcasts, habitually informing us we would amount to nothing, which crushed my self-esteem. The vile my stepfather spewed though, willed me to be successful. Raymond and I were really all each other had. This realization cemented our bond.

My stepfather's brother attempted to molest me and that's when I realized that monsters were real. I defended myself against his touch, but I told my uncle, Buster, what he tried to do to me. Uncle Buster promptly beat his ass and that guy could not come near us again. As an adult, I have defeated those monsters I thought were much too strong. It turns out I am stronger than what tries to consume me. No matter what life throws your way, you can accomplish something great. I'm a witness to that.

One day, enough was enough when it came to the beatings. According to Aunt Stein the look on my face spoke volumes and even she knew I was fed up. I gave my stepfather a look one day and threatened him with any words I could muster up. I was never beaten by him again.

There were a few good men that impacted my life in more ways than I can count. Frederick J. Richards surprised our fourth-grade class with a visit and a moving speech. He was a good-looking, stately, light-skinned man who wore a very nice suit and tie. He may have looked like a city official to other kids, but to me, he looked like Superman, and I wanted to be like him. My stepfather didn't wear a suit unless he was going to church. Mr. Richards spoke to us, lighting up the room with his voice. I wanted to wear a suit and tie and have charisma that excites a room just like him. It was the first time I thought about what I wanted to do when I grew up.

I learned that Mr. Richards was running for office

and eventually became the first African American elected to Congress in Mississippi. He was also the first African American to hold the position as the United States Secretary of Agriculture. I enjoyed his speech so much that I researched him and asked questions about him. I learned he was into martial arts. To this day, I'm into martial arts. Meeting him in elementary school planted the seed and the desire to accomplish more in my life. I realized I wanted to be more than my surroundings.

Sometime later I had the opportunity to go to Mr. Richards's office. There was a picture there that I will never forget. It was an image of him walking down the Great Wall of China. I couldn't imagine someone from Mississippi going to China. It seemed so far off from my reality, but it wasn't.

After I met Mr. Richards, I paid closer attention to my environment. I wanted to one day be as successful as he. I watched the things the adults in my life did to survive. I learned from observation. I knew hard-working folks in my community, and some people had nice homes and cars. I wanted that, but I had to take some different paths to get there.

Several years later, we moved into a three-bedroom house. This was significant because, before we moved into our new home, we lived with extended family members and in a few different apartment complexes. There were sometimes during the week that I didn't spend the night at the same house twice in a row. Since we left

Jackson, this was the first time we weren't sharing space with any extended family members.

Finally, we were settled in a place we could call home. Although I'm grateful for all the circumstances my siblings and I have endured, it was a complete game-changer once we moved into this house. My mother worked multiple jobs to keep food on the table and the lights on. I walked into the Social Services office with Mom on multiple occasions. We needed all the help we could get.

Consequently, our circumstances made us entrepreneurs. There was a pecan tree in our backyard where it seemed an endless supply of pecans grew. During the holidays, my brother and I gathered pecans and sold them for one dollar per bag.

We made sure our prices were less than the dollar store where we hustled them. We had a system that worked nicely. I picked the pecans, and my brother packed them, while our mother supplied the bags. Since the customers loved fresh pecans, they formed a line outside the store to purchase from us. The money we made was a nice addition to our seemingly empty coin banks. Sometimes, we made enough money to buy a pair of shoes we liked.

Our pecan hustle lasted for two years. Once that business venture ended, my older brother and I maintained neighbors' lawns for extra cash. I knew the value of arduous work and earning your own money. I just didn't realize there were other things I picked up, too, that I'd eventually have to unlearn.

I reflected on these things (the first 16 years of my life) while I recovered in the hospital. As angry as I was, I didn't want to leave the family that I cared so deeply for. I was grateful to be alive and I channeled all the anger I was feeling into work.

CHAPTER 3

WORKING DAY AND NIGHT

It was at Chastain Middle School, between 1989-1990, that I realized Jackson was a lot like Canton. I was skinny, but tough and the muscles I did have at that age helped my punches to serve a severe impact. Just like in Canton, I was defending myself from big kids who wanted to pick on me. I knew eventually, I would have to make an example of someone if I was going to prove I could hold my own. "Hold up or fold up," is what they used to say in Canton. It didn't help that I was also getting a lot of attention from the girls being the new kid in school. Mom always kept us fresh, with clean clothes and new shoes. Yet, I was still dealing with low self-esteem from the bullying endured before arriving in Jackson.

I spent most of my middle and high school years involved in physical altercations with other students. My grades were above average, but my focus wasn't on academics. Other superficial things competed for my attention just like any other teenage boy in the 90's. I wanted to be the best dresser. I also wanted to be popular in my class. I didn't realize I was seeking the validation I wasn't getting at home.

My situation at home was still rocky because Mom

was once again in communication with her estranged husband. I knew another change was on its way. Shortly thereafter, I left Chastain and transferred to Powell Middle School. I skipped school often and had a little bit too much fun with the girls in school. While it was enjoyable, my teenage libido got me into a lot of trouble.

The growing number of gangs that infiltrated most of Jackson caused me to live in survival mode every day. This unexpected dynamic changed my entire attitude. I limited my conversations with the girls to avoid conflict with the guys. Whenever I had an opportunity to spend time with a girl, I would go to her home, naturally, while her parents were at work. Seemed like a solid enough plan, but it didn't always work the way I imagined.

I recall one time a group of guys robbed and beat me while I was walking through a neighborhood to visit one of my girlfriends. A blue car pulled up, four guys jumped out, and pointed a gun at my chest. They demanded I take off my Chicago Bulls Starter jacket and my sneakers. When I snapped out of the initial shock, I discovered that I knew one kid – a dropout from my school.

This was the second time someone pointed a gun at me. I took off my jacket first and as soon as I bent down to take off my shoes, one of them kicked me from behind and I fell to the ground. I was being kicked from all angles until they got my shoes off my feet. When it was over, I got up with a busted lip and a few bumps on my head. I never made it to my girlfriend's house. I didn't want her to see me like that.

I brushed myself off and headed down Bishop Avenue where I lived. On the way home, an OG asked what happened to me. So, I told him. He stopped me in the middle of the story and asked me to get the full name of the guy who jumped on me once I returned to school. I did exactly what he asked. A few days later, I picked up my things from the principal's office and it was never spoken of again. One of those guys had the ass-whooping of a lifetime. Years later, I learned that one of those guys was shot and, after several crimes, yet another ended up in jail. The guys in the neighborhood saw me as a harmless little boy and not a threat to them.

Working has always been a means of power for me. When I was a teenager, it enabled me to focus on something other than home and school. I could also provide a better quality of life for myself. My work experiences made me the professional I am today, while the streets made me a man. When I was younger, I really wanted to be a doctor or a lawyer. I knew both required a college education, but I didn't know exactly how to go about achieving that goal. There weren't many examples in my neighborhood to imitate concerning higher education.

My mother didn't have a college degree, but I wouldn't dare say she was an uneducated woman, as that is far from the truth. She earned certifications and licenses to be a nurse's assistant and a hairstylist. So even though I didn't know much about college yet, one thing I did know was that I needed to start working somewhere soon.

I started mowing lawns for six or seven dollars a yard. I pursued as many opportunities as I possibly could. Once I received a work permit, I immediately hit the streets in search of a steady income. Although I missed most school functions, dances, and basketball games, I never let that faze me. My mother worked hard and we saw the benefits of that daily. She worked multiple jobs to feed and clothe her family. I learned a great deal from her work ethic.

I spent some time working as a server's assistant and waiter at restaurants like El Chicos, Bennigan's, Sbarro's and Olive Garden. One particularly memorable and challenging night stands out in my recollection. It was a bustling Friday evening in 1998 and the restaurant was packed with hungry diners eager to start their weekend with a delicious meal. As soon as I clocked in for my shift it became apparent that the night was going to be a whirlwind. Tables were filling up rapidly and the kitchen staff was struggling to keep up with the high demand. Orders were pouring in from every direction and the hustle and bustle in the dining area was at fever pitch.

With each passing minute, the intensity grew. My ability to multitask and remain composed was put to the ultimate test. Balancing multiple trays, navigating through crowded aisles, and ensuring orders were delivered accurately and promptly felt like an adrenaline-fueled dance. To complicate matters, unexpected challenges arose throughout the night. One table had a customer with severe food allergies, requiring extra care and attention to prevent any cross-contamination. Another group was celebrating a special occasion, demanding my involvement in orchestrating surprises and coordinating with the kitchen and other staff members. Despite the chaos and pressure, I maintained a calm demeanor and worked tirelessly to provide exceptional service to each customer.

I relied on my training, experience, and ability to think on my feet to overcome obstacles, prioritize tasks, and maintain a positive attitude. By the end of the night, I was physically and mentally exhausted, but also filled with a sense of accomplishment. The night of the never-ending rush taught me the value of resilience, adaptability, and teamwork. It solidified my passion for providing exceptional customer service, even in the face of challenging circumstances.

By the time I was a junior in high school, I spent a lot of my time working at Triple C, a full-service body shop and car wash, in Jackson. I thrived there because not only did I make money from my hourly wage, but I also received heavy tips from the car owners. BMWs, Lexus Coupes, Corvettes, and, my favorite, Cadillac on twenty-twos were all the rage back in the 1990s when I was a teenager and I wanted one of them as soon as I could afford it. Can you blame me?

In the hood, cars were a sign of wealth. Luxury vehicles set the tone. It seemed like all gangsters and hustlers wanted to do was make sure their vehicles were clean and gleaming when they rolled through the city. In the words of Curtis Mayfield, they were "digging the scene with the gangster lean," with one arm hanging out of the window.

After months of saving and researching, I finally found the perfect car—a sleek, 2-door, black Ford Escort, which made me feel a sense of pride and independence. I cherished the freedom it provided and the adventures I envisioned taking with it.

Motivated by money, I entered the Teen Youth Center Club in the neighborhood to inquire about a job. The supervisor there informed me they were not hiring. I went back to them every day to ask if they were hiring. At night, on the weekends, the Center turned into sort of a club for teens. It was like the "High Life" on the TV sitcom, "South Central." If I worked there, I knew I could get in for free.

Finally, one day, the supervisor threw her hands up in surrender and announced, "This young man has come in here every single day determined to work. I'm going to have to fire one of my other employees and give him a job!" She took me under her wing and taught me things no other person in my life could. Our relationship grew from supervisor and subordinate to godmother and godson. Before the year was over, I was living with my new

Godmom full-time.

Godmom was my motivation to complete my education. School and work became my top priorities. Sometimes, this placed me at odds with my family. They felt I abandoned them. I was the Black Sheep early on, which is someone who grows beyond expectations of others or their environment, and I could never shake the label, even now.

I worked at both the Youth Center and the car wash, while maintaining my grades in school. I felt like things were looking up for my future. Fortunately, I didn't get too caught up in all the dealings of the gangsters whose cars I cleaned. I drove for them from time to time and parked them in designated areas. One guy, in particular, who was quite notably one of the most powerful men on the streets, also happened to be one of the wisest men I knew. He took me under his wing and entrusted me with his knowledge of life in Jacktown.

If I learned anything from dealing with him and some of the other car owners, it was how to build character and not to lie to people. I learned to never turn my back on people and to be there for others. I learned to just be good to folks. To treat others how I would want them to treat me. Of course, I eventually also discovered that just because you are good to people doesn't mean they will be good to you.

I found out the hard way that sometimes you just couldn't trust everyone; people will lie to you even when you are good to them. The streets educated me. They taught me that just because I wouldn't harm anyone doesn't mean they won't harm me.

I was thirteen years old when death affected me the first time. JJ's best friend, Isaiah, was quiet and soft-spoken. He didn't belong to a gang, nor did he sell drugs. We had just finished playing basketball and began heading home. Someone killed him shortly after we went our separate ways. He died at seventeen years old. That was Mississippi in the 1990s.

We lost a lot of friends during our formative years. Some to the drug game, others to senseless violence that had nothing to do with them. Isaiah's death was a prelude to the wave of violence that claimed so many lives. There were at least fifteen to twenty people I knew who were here one day and gone the next. There was a song by the rap group UGK entitled, "One Day." The lyrics were appropriate: "One day you're here the next day you're gone." This song resonated with me. It played like a soundtrack in my head throughout my teenage years, but I had to keep pushing.

I held over twenty different jobs through my junior and senior years in high school. I learned to seize opportunities and worked in every place that hired me. I worked so hard, I rarely played (except for a little basketball here and there) but, of course, the ladies were an ever-present distraction.

The Jitney Jungle was a local grocery store, during

my teen years where I gained an awareness of managerial and people skills. This was one of the most memorable places I worked. Mr. Tim, a six-foot-three White male, was the manager. The owners of the store lived nearby in a mansion. Tim was the most fun manager to work for. He allowed me to open the store in the mornings and on the weekend. He trusted me with the keys to the store. Shortly thereafter, I became the middle manager. Cashiers and baggers brought minor issues to me before they reached Tim, who took me under his wing. He showed me how to count and deposit money. Everything related to the grocery store, I learned from Tim.

Unfortunately, it all ended when Tim moved out of state for another position with another company. The owner of Jitney Jingle hired a tall Black woman. She gave me hell. There were times when I felt undervalued and ignored, as if my contributions and concerns were inconsequential. That was the beginning of me being fired by women of color. I felt it was a curse that every woman who hired me fired me. Especially those who showed attraction toward me, and I showed them no interest, even if I was slightly intrigued. Eventually, she was convicted of stealing money from the company, which shattered any remaining trust and respect that might have lingered. It was hard, but despite the challenges I faced with her, I tried to remember not to let one person define my perception of an entire group. Every individual is unique, and the actions of one person should not cast a negative shadow on others who share the same characteristics or identity.

Although it sounds strange, these women have taught me a great deal about myself. I learned how to visualize things differently while working for women. I also learned a lot about the importance of clear communication. They showed me how to observe from another's perspective.

One Saturday morning while I was on the clock, Mandy, a blond, cheerleader who was five foot, nine came into the store. I was kind of feeling her and she must have liked me, too, because she kept coming back while I was there to torment me with the cans in the aisle. I would purposely turn the canned goods in the opposite direction and burst into laughter, all while saying, "You missed this one." We would both laugh.

This went on for about two weeks until one day she asked me to help her take the groceries to her car. I'll never forget that short cheerleader skirt and those thick-ass thighs. She had a way of looking at me with blue eyes that turned me on. After I put her groceries in the car, she asked for my phone number, and she gave me hers. That was the beginning of our relationship.

Mandy challenged me to confront any biases or stereotypes I held. Our relationship encouraged me to have more open dialogue about race, privilege, and equality. In a fleeting time, I gained a better understanding of the importance of empathy, cultural sensitivity, and the value of diverse perspectives. In the south, there was still a great deal of stereotyping people of different races. It was not a common idea that interracial relationships could be healthy, loving, and meaningful. It was also hard to believe that people could have things in common with people who were of different ethnicities. However, I spent evenings at Mandy's house, helping her with some cheerleading moves. It was then that I learned her mom was a working parent like my mom and Mandy was an only child.

First loves often hold a special place in our hearts, as they introduce us to the excitement, joy, and sometimes heartache that comes with romantic relationships. One day, Mandy told me she was pregnant. After discussing it, we decided an abortion was best. We broke up for a while and got back together, and then she moved away. I never saw her again. After Mandy, there was a Dominican girl, who was new to our school, named Alisa. After Alisa, there were many more, but none of them topped the one that came with the opportunity of a lifetime.

The choir at school received an invitation to travel throughout Europe to perform at various venues. I planned on shadowing the choir. I knew Mom couldn't afford this trip, and I didn't want to ask Godmom for the money. Luckily, I didn't have to ask anyone for anything. I had all these jobs so, naturally, my earnings afforded me more than enough to go on the trip.

After I moved in, Godmom married my godfather,

Cody, who had become like a father to me. To my delight, Cody was a good man. He married Godmom and agreed to her conditions that my godbrother and I came as a package deal. Cody never treated me with anger, and for that, I am blessed. He taught me everything within his power and showed me genuine concern (without the barbarity I experienced with my stepfather,) of which, I appreciated. He advised me to save my money instead of investing it on the trip. He was big on saving money and investing. Godmom, however, had a different point of view.

"Go on the trip! Travel is the only thing you can spend money on and be enriched," she countered. She was from a more progressive, educated family who traveled. She didn't want me to miss out on a great opportunity because of my anxious thoughts or Cody's.

I'm grateful I listened to her. I had never been to a place as different as Europe. It felt surreal for a young kid from Jackson, Mississippi. My first time on a plane was a trip that took me halfway around the world. That trip abroad took me to Normandy, Germany, England, France, and Norway. I toured places I thought I would only see inside my schoolbooks. We took a boat ride across the English Channel and spent time on the Beaches of Normandy. They will take your breath away. The water was crystal clear and the sand was pristine.

I fell in love with the rich history, beautiful architecture, lovely accents, and delicious food. Admittedly, that wasn't all I fell in love with. I indulged in a few extracurricular activities while in Paris, thanks to Annie, who traveled with us on the school trip. She kept flirting with me on the plane and while we were transitioning to our hotel. Annie was a beautiful young lady with a bright smile, curly red hair, and a cute bubble butt. We became fast friends on the trip.

On one of our excursions, we played sick to stay behind to have a little fun. We went back to our rooms at separate times until the coast was clear to see each other. My hotel phone rang, and she was on the other end. What can I say? I was a teenager with raging hormones and no parental supervision.

She said, "I'm coming over."

"Okay."

I showered, brushed my teeth, and made sure I had the music right and condoms in the nightstand. When she got to my room, she was wearing a short, red mini dress. She went to the window, bent over to reach for the curtains, and, to my surprise, she wasn't wearing panties. I followed her and lifted her dress. With her hands on the window, I reached into my pocket while I pulled my pants off. We were two horny teenagers, making love while staring at the Eiffel Tower. I was enamored by the views outside and inside the room. We knew we had about two to three hours, so we didn't rush.

We promised each other we would keep our tryst a secret. I should have known better. Our secret lasted a tad longer than the transcontinental flight home. Annie confided our secret to her friends, and the news traveled at rapid speed. Meanwhile, Annie called to say she might be pregnant. All the homies were praising the hell out of me. It scared me, though. After a few weeks of waiting, she reached out to me and said it was a false alarm. Talk about being relieved! Every time I thought about our trip abroad, Annie crossed my mind. The memories we shared throughout that two-week journey were priceless.

Don't get me wrong; the Eiffel Tower, Notre Dame Cathedral, and the Palace of Versailles were sites to behold for young Black man, too. I was even shocked to see the bidet and the urinal amenities in my bathroom. It took me a moment to figure out how Europeans cleaned up after they used the restroom. I learned more about the world during that trip than I ever learned inside a classroom. The trip had a lasting impact and international travel has become a permanent part of my life.

Back at home, it was almost graduation time. It was 1995 and I was preparing for my last high school year, enjoying my new car, and having the fun time all seniors should have. My friends and I decided we should go to Mardi Gras that year and I decided to drive. We spared no expense and broke all the rules teenage boys like to break! It's easier to ask me what we didn't do than for me to tell you what we did.

You don't go to Mardi Gras without dancing in the middle of the street like all the visitors and locals were doing. Everyone was drinking, eating, and partying all up and down the French Quarter. Women were dressed in slinky clothes and bright colors. Bars were open with all kinds of music blasting from every other door. Beads were being thrown everywhere! At 12:30 a.m., it was time to go. We headed back up the highway toward Jackson, excited, and talking about graduation and high school memories. That conversation lasted until we arrived in the city and I dropped everyone off safely.

Since it was way past my curfew, I decided I wanted to spend the night at my mother's house. As I was driving home, I stopped at the light near my mother's street. Once I crept through the light, a car drove head-on toward my car, sending me straight into a neighbor's ditch. The car motor was almost in my lap. The entire front windshield had landed on my forehead. I ended up in the hospital with a punctured liver and spleen. The impact left my right eye scarred and damaged for life. I had to get stitches in my eye and was in a deep coma for several days. "You're lucky to be alive," the doctor said, emphatically. I had almost died again!

I started reflecting on our trip to New Orleans. "That was too much fun," I admitted, silently to myself, "Never again!" In the car, my friend, Al, kept asking me, "Do you want to chill at the spot after the long drive?" I turned him down three times. In the hospital, I kept hearing Godmom's voice saying, "After 12 AM, stay where you are." I should have stayed in New Orleans, but I didn't realize how exhausted I really was. A hard head makes a soft ass.

I'll admit I learned some lessons from that trip. Listen to those who care about you and know you well. They have wisdom that can save your life. Don't overextend yourself with anything. Drinking and smoking in excess can harm you in ways you may live to regret or die from. Lastly, grown up things are for grown up people. I wish I hadn't been in such a rush to grow up.

High school had its ups and downs, and I was looking forward to it being over. Unfortunately, I wasn't well enough to attend graduation. Like most teenagers, graduation was an important thing for me. However, being alive meant so much more. My school lost a lot of kids over drunk driving and drugs. I thought I was going to be in that number... God had a different plan.

CHAPTER 4

COLLEGE BOY

A mail order high school diploma wasn't quite how I envisioned my graduation experience to end. The entire situation with my accident replayed in my head a thousand times as I lay in the hospital. Even weeks after I was discharged, I couldn't believe how much pain I was in after what I thought was such a great night. In the end, the accident became a pivotal moment in my car ownership journey. It reminded me of the fragility of life and the importance of cherishing the things we hold dear.

I looked at my damaged vehicle before the insurance company took possession of it—twisted, torn, and mangled. Somehow, the look of the car reminded me of my state of mind. I wanted a better life so, clearly, it was time for a change. Godmom must have felt the same thing I was feeling because, instinctively, she took me to see her brother, Uncle D.

Uncle D was a well-educated, Black man who believed in uplifting young people. The first time we met, I wasted milk on his blazer when I got in the car. I was not ready for the stern lecture, with cursing, that I received for that. "Young man, I'm disappointed in you. You need to be more careful and responsible for your damn actions!" He conveyed his feelings with such a serious demeanor, I think I teared up a little bit. Talk about crying over spilled milk! He later apologized for being over-the-top about it because he knew it was an accident, but by then his words had already left a lasting impression on me. He laughed it off and told me it was alright. That was the beginning of our twenty-plus-year relationship.

Godmom and I stopped by Jackson State University one evening to speak with Uncle D about some business. After a while, he directed his attention towards me. "Are you going to attend college? What are you planning on doing with your life?" he interrogated me with that spilled milk voice. My heart dropped to the bottom of my feet. Life had just gotten real! Although I thought I was doing well in high school, it wasn't good enough for college admission. Once I was exposed to the idea, I couldn't help but consider it further. "Bring him to my office tomorrow," he instructed Godmom, who was all too ready to hand me over.

While I was excited about the possibility of attending college, I was nervous about the application process and anxious about the school's response. But Uncle D provided valuable guidance and support during the entire process. First, he helped me navigate the complexities of the application, including gathering required documents, filling out forms, and understanding deadlines.

In addition to emotional support, Uncle D shared practical knowledge and insights about college in general. He provided advice on selecting schools, crafting compelling personal statements, and he even helped me prepare for interviews. Learning from his experiences and expertise, I gained a deeper understanding of what colleges were looking for and how to present myself effectively on the application. I applied for grants and student loans, as well.

I didn't know about any of these things. Uncle D eased any anxieties I had and made the process feel more manageable. I felt reassured and encouraged by his involvement. He was the perfect mentor. I vowed to be an encourager and an example for others just like him.

As I anxiously checked the mail, I received a letter from the college admissions office. The realization that it held the news I had been eagerly awaiting sank in. The envelope felt heavy in my hands, carrying the potential to shape my future. I found a quiet spot, and, with bated breath, I opened the envelope. Time seemed to slow down as I read the words that confirmed my acceptance into college. A wave of relief, joy, and accomplishment washed over me, accompanied by an electric surge of excitement.

In that moment, the weight of my hard work, dedication, and the support of my loved ones came to fruition. It was a turning point, marking the beginning of a new chapter in my life. I couldn't help but feel a profound sense of pride in achieving this significant milestone. Eager to share the news, I reached out to my family and friends, who had been on this journey with me. The joy and celebrations that followed were a testament to the collective effort and support that had brought me to this point. Before I knew it, with a few grants and student loans, I was enrolled into Jackson State University.

Before the first day I walked the halls of Jackson State University, I had to learn how to dress differently. Uncle D modeled accountability, discipline, and perseverance in every way. He introduced me to the "dress code of life." Yes, I grew up wearing tennis shoes, but wearing dress shoes, suits, and ties became a norm for me on campus. My uncle coached me on how to prepare and dress for interviews, lessons I would use for the rest of my life. Cody showed me love and how life can be on the streets and Uncle D showed me the way of life off the streets.

My uncle made sure I learned that just because I made a mistake it didn't mean I was out of the ballgame. "Just pick up where you left off and keep it moving," he would say. He confessed that he, too, had a few run-ins with the law and troubles throughout his career also. I didn't realize I'd received the very same lessons Uncle D learned real-life situations until I ran into them. I have the utmost respect for Uncle D; I would go to war for him. He made me see a better me! If it weren't for God-mom introducing me to him, I probably wouldn't be where I am today. He changed my life and Jackson State was the new chapter I needed.

JSU was the perfect place for me to spread my wings

and grow. Imagine not thinking you're ready or qualified for college and then being voted "Mr. Freshman". It was a surreal moment indeed. I didn't know much about homecoming courts. It was a like spin-off of what we did in high school with class queens and kings. One day, I was coming from class dressed head-to-toe in Polo. A group of girls walked up to me and asked, "Would you like to run for Mr. Freshman?"

"I'm already fresh!" I smirked; a little confidence never hurt anyone.

They started laughing and then explained what it was. If I ran and won, I would represent the entire freshman class.

I paused for a beat and said, "Sign me up!"

The young ladies said I needed to get one hundred signatures to make the ballot. I paused again and my brain took off, so to speak. They saw it in my eyes and started convincing me to just do it. Talk about peer pressure! That very moment led to the birth of the politician within. I rallied my classmates to gather signatures, which quickly made me an eligible candidate. I politely requested their support, which they quickly agreed to. The mission was on and we accomplished that goal within five hours.

This was my first time learning how to develop a point of view, share it with constituents and influence voters. This group became my first campaign team on the trail. I knocked each contender off the map, one by one, until we had the last opponent. I became "Mr. Freshman" by a landslide. I was overjoyed about the victory and hosted a pizza party for my team.

"Party" became a bigger word in my life than "class" as it does with many first-year students. It's hard to adjust to having a certain level of freedom. Nobody is going to wake you up and make you go to class. Nobody is going to make you study or go to the library. You must do it because you want to. By the end of my freshman year, my grades were suffering, and I knew why. I was too busy trying to make money and chasing women. Going into my sophomore year, I had to buckle down to get my grades back up or face getting kicked out of school. I didn't want to disappoint Uncle D, nor myself.

University life increased my self-esteem and morale. It was a whole other world – literally. People came from around the globe to attend Jackson State University. It was an exhilarating time. I had moved onto campus after moving out of Godmom's house. As I settled inside the dorm, I noticed I was happy and smiling from ear-to-ear. Even though this was all new to me, it was electrifying. I was looking forward to seeing what more college life had to offer. However, my street life wasn't too far away.

I kept my connections with Red, one of the biggest drug dealers in Mississippi, whose car I drove from time-to-time. I still worked and hung out at the car wash between classes. I hung out with Red because he was very smart and took a liking to me. I listened to his words of wisdom. He was another a big brother, father, and mentor to me all at the same time. For reasons unknown to me, he was protecting me all the time, no matter where I was. Red cared that I was going to college. The bond he showed me around the other dope boys was deep. Even though they called me "College Boy," they all respected me. I was one of a few students in our neighborhood who had higher aspirations outside of the streets.

Unfortunately, someone murdered Red while I was at JSU in 1998. The DEA found several kilos in his garage. I was no longer untouchable, and I knew I had to get out of Jackson soon or lay low. As I reflected on Red's sudden death, my mind snapped back to being shot at the basketball court. Did my association with the dealers contribute to that attack? I couldn't rule out if that was a possible reason. The police never found the shooter. I think about that a lot. Is my attempted killer still out there, or has he met the same fate he tried to deal my way?

I saved the money I made from all my jobs, remained low-key, and focused on my studies. Watching the same sad affair play out constantly was a miserable occurrence, but it reminded me of what I needed to focus on: working and finishing college. I couldn't afford any distractions. In the 1990s, beepers were the hottest technology. My godparents owned a pager company that I started working at periodically just before I graduated high school. I spent more time there than at the car wash after a while. It was the safest thing to do at the time.

I was also in the drama club during my sophomore year. There was an award named after Paul Laurence Dunbar and I was selected to receive the "Mr. Dramatic Dunbar Gill" award. I represented the entire Arts department during that year. I was also a part of the "Insatiable Modeling Squad." It was a club on campus that showcased clothing, accessories, and other products through posing and photography for advertising campaigns, fashion shows, or other promotional purposes. I didn't know these types of activities existed in college. The people I met in these groups made the campus experience much easier to navigate.

I had three roommates getting acclimated with me to this new environment of living among strangers, but we worked it out by establishing some rules and boundaries. Or so we thought. One day, two of my roommates and I returned to the room to freshen up. There were women all over campus and we were ready to get our mack on. Instantly, that excitement disappeared when we saw our ransacked room. Someone had robbed us!

We looked at each other and called for security. Everyone had multiple items missing. Then, we noticed all the belongings of one of our roommates were gone. It turned out he had robbed all of us and never returned to school. An old feeling resurfaced. I was ready for revenge, but we couldn't find him. I had just purchased an expensive watch, and I wanted it back. After that fiasco, it was time for me to move off-campus. I rented a one-bedroom apartment near the school. Not too long after that, Godmom's mother offered me the opportunity to stay in a three-bedroom house. I was relieved. I couldn't trust anyone. Was this how the rest of my college life would be? I really wanted to embrace the full higher education experience, but I spent most of my time navigating life, not the university.

Over time, I fell back in love with the university atmosphere. During my junior year I pledged Alpha Phi Alpha Fraternity, Incorporated. The community service and other activities of the fraternity helped to keep me in positive circles during what little spare time I had. The frat gave me experience with voter engagement, mentoring at local schools, tutoring at libraries, and participating in elder care. From time to time, I thought about what my life would have been like, with my brothers and my sister, if I had stayed home after getting shot.

In my downtime, between classes or late at night, I thought about my siblings. Our lives were vastly different, and we knew it. Often, I felt that they held that against me. Whether that was true or not, I tried not to let it bother me because I knew our bond was unbreakable. There was even a time I allowed my brothers and family members to live with me for a stint, supporting them to save money and become financially stable.

College taught me about other cultures, how they lived, and took care of one another. Unfortunately, I learned the hard way that some members of my family only wanted to buy more clothes and spend money on women. It was becoming too much to deal with under one roof. You can't help everybody, not even those closest to you sometimes. So, they slowly departed from my house. Once that ended, I continued to focus on school and working.

For a few months, I worked as a cashier at the local Kroger grocery store. Most of the customers who came through the grocery store went to Jackson State University. I developed lasting friendships while working there, and it added another layer of customer service to my resume. Mr. Richards also helped me get a job as a Tennis Court Assistant at a local country club, where I collected tennis balls after each match. I didn't know there was such a position until I applied. As I watched the tennis matches and read up on the rules, I learned a great deal about the game and developed a strong appreciation for tennis.

I didn't start thinking about a career versus jobs until I was introduced to the United States Department of Agriculture (USDA) in Mississippi. There are very few occupations in Mississippi that can support and sustain one's way of life, and one of those entities is the federal government. Working for the government in Mississippi is a stable position. I worked in the public affairs office for the Natural Resources Conservation Service (NRCS) as a GS-1. A Black man ran the department I worked for,

Agricultural Marketing Services. He was high in rank within the USDA.

I never imagined a Black man being over anything governmental, especially in Mississippi. He had a distinguished career and was well respected for his experience in the industry. He was known for being charismatic, inspiring, and supportive. When we first met during the hiring process, he gave me a firm handshake and said, "I believe in you and I want you to do a great job." I appreciated him for investing time in me and not just expressing his belief in me. It was a terrific opportunity and I loved it. It felt good to know another seasoned Black man supported me. But just like with any job, the USDA came with its difficulties.

Working with the federal government was cumbersome and sometimes very confusing. There was a lot of bureaucracy and things that I didn't understand. To get over the tough times, I volunteered to wear character costumes and explain certain things about agriculture to middle school and high school students. This was a way of teaching them they could seek employment within the government. It was the Agency's way of giving back to the community.

One of the highlights of my JSU experience was receiving an invitation to Costa Rica for a student study abroad program. Along with several other Jackson State University students, I signed up to live in Costa Rica for a semester. This was the pilot year for the study abroad program, and we were excited to take part. We had to finance our trip, which was fine for me. My godfather encouraged me to be more of a saver than a spender. I saved a great deal of money from my jobs and was ready for the trip. Even though I had enough money from the loans and grants, the hustler in me never died. I worked in Jackson State's biology department as well to save up extra money to cover my expenses.

My first month in Costa Rica was a culture shock. My host family, the Enriques, were a beautiful family that accepted me as one of their own. The couple had a six-year-old boy and an eight-year-old girl who became my siblings while I lived there. Each morning, I awakened to my little brother staring at me. Right after he left, my little sister would come running through the door full of excitement. I thought it was weird, but she reminded me of my little sister back home.

My thoughts vacillated between concern for my family and the beautiful environment that surrounded me. Worlds apart, the thought of my sister laid heavy on my heart. I thought about her and prayed for her, but I knew God was protecting her. We had seen little of each other since I was in college. At times I felt I had abandoned her. Then, I would snap back to reality and remember I was in Costa Rica. I vowed to make this experience as memorable as possible.

Mornings with the Enrique family began with breakfast: eggs, bread, and green plantains pounded into small fritters and fried into Patacones, which are irresistible when dipped in refried beans. This became a part of my daily diet. From time to time, I would venture out to the local markets to try other dishes.

My "madre" and "padre" turned out to be the coolest. They were all about love and family. Padre attempted to teach me more Spanish and reduce my anxieties about living abroad. For instance, I was unfamiliar with the local transportation system and getting around in a new country is challenging. The bus rides around the mountains were like being in an Indiana Jones movie you never knew if the bus was going to fall off the side of the mountain. The air was always dusty and I was always scared if the bus driver could see. However, my padre assured me that we would make it to our destination safely and we did.

His mother would visit the house often and, when she did, she would rub my hair for over fifteen minutes every time. I never understood why, but it didn't make me feel uncomfortable. The family was all there looking, laughing, and waiting for a reaction from me. I would just smile. It reminded me of how Aunt Stein used to rub and brush the waves into my hair each night after we finished praying.

At times, I felt quite spoiled by the Enriques. They also had a housekeeper. I didn't have to wash, cook, or clean after myself and that's not something you want to get too used to when you're a young man. My Costa Rican family helped me realize that family is really all you have in this world. I learned to treasure every moment I had with them, reflecting on how I would treat my own family when I returned home.

Though my Spanish family was very hospitable, I spent most of my time touring the countryside of Costa Rica. In the rainforest I saw strange, poisonous frogs of many colors. I saw the toothpaste tree, a little evergreen shrub that contains antibacterial properties that can kill the bad bacteria in our mouths and fight bad breath. Also, I visited a banana farm. Of all the areas I visited, Puerto Limon is one place I will never forget. It's largely known for its Creole and Black population. It is by far the most culturally diverse province in Costa Rica.

Limon is both the name of the province and the capital city. I stayed in a cabin that sat above the forest tree lines. Looking out of the windows into Veragua Rainforest Park was breathtaking. The greenery expanded across the sky. It was one of the most beautiful scenic views I've ever experienced. During the evenings, I heard monkeys and birds calling out to one another. The feeling was surreal. I was experiencing this all because I had the courage to leave home and I wasn't the only one.

Students from Australia, the United Kingdom, and West Africa attended the Institute of Costa Rica. I made lots of friends from all over the world who I still communicate with to this day. We would meet up for coffee or tea or visit nightspots where loud music played well into the early morning. Though all of us had ventured out on excursions, school was most important and surprisingly fun. We immersed ourselves in Costa Rican culture. During those moments, I released all the worries that came with living in Mississippi. Timothy, Akbar, and Shila were my "compadres" and nothing could tear us apart. Though I never became fluent in Spanish after leaving Costa Rica, the memory of us trying to become fluent would remain dear to my heart.

I heard Spanish is one of the most romantic languages, but I didn't expect to fall in love in Costa Rica. I mean, I fell deeply and madly in love and I fell hard. When I met Alanna, everything moved in slow motion. I experienced an LL Cool J moment, reminiscent of "Round the Way Girl." I was on my way home and she was standing at the bus stop, drinking soda pop. Her hair was long, jet-black, and hung down her back. It just so happened we were getting on a packed bus. I made sure I put two pieces of gum in my mouth before I said anything to her. I was in the beginning stages of learning certain Spanish words, but I knew enough to ask for her name and tell her mine. She started smiling and speaking slowly. Her voice was so sexy and soothing, it made my heart skip a beat. We continued our conversation until it was time to get off the bus.

I saw her again a few days later at the same bus stop. She majored in Molecular and Cellular Biology at the University of Costa Rica. I had another friend with me at the time; he lived along the same bus route. He had been in the country longer than I had and was more fluent in Spanish, so he translated everything I wanted to tell her. Thanks to him, she gave me her number, and we became fast friends.

Alanna became my tour guide. Like everyone else, she was friendly and took pride in teaching me things about her home. The locals showed no signs of trouble or disrespect toward me. After we visited parts of the city, she would make sure I got home safely. The relationship became deeper the more time we shared. Then one day, she invited me to her home and made sweet love to me, while speaking in her native tongue. Our relationship grew with each passing day. I was infatuated, but I grew to genuinely love Alanna.

Between the beauty of Costa Rica and the enchanting women, I was hooked. Alanna was just as fun as she was beguiling. I spent so much time with her that my host family wondered if I would ever make it through the door some nights. "I'm learning and practicing the language," I said sheepishly, one night. My padre started laughing, "Oh si, mijo ... el idioma!" He knew what was up. I was practicing a whole lot more than the language!

When the semester was over and it was time to leave, I wasn't ready. Alanna and I both cried like babies at the Juan Santamaría airport. I wasn't sure if I would ever return, but I knew in my heart that was the first time I felt genuine love. Kissing her goodbye was the hardest thing I ever had to do with a girl. We continued our communications for months into another year, which came to end because I didn't want to lead her on. We mutually came to an understanding. If the universe should allow it, we will meet again.

I was aware of the impact Costa Rica and Alanna had on me. I witnessed a veritable paradise, and I wanted to see more of it. I knew what that required. I had to change my focus from looking successful to becoming a success. I had lofty dreams and goals I knew would take me out of my comfort zone, but I was willing and ready for the change.

The street life and hustling paid the bills, but there was no retirement or 401(k) plan with that life. I learned by watching my friends. None of them worked at traditional jobs. They hustled to make ends meet. I knew deep down inside I needed to make a change if I wanted to see my forties. The thought of it all hit me hard because Mississippi was my home, but to grow, I needed to leave it behind.

In 1999, I graduated from Jackson State University with a Bachelor of Arts in Speech Communication. I was the first person in my family to earn a college degree. I was proud of this achievement and even more proud that my sister and, eventually, my younger brother, Ray, would follow in my footsteps.

Since I worked for the USDA in Mississippi, I could successfully transfer to the Washington, D.C., office. I put in a transfer request with the USDA and I was ecstatic when the approval came through. The day after graduation I bought a brand-new green 1999 Ford Escort. Then, I took every dime I made from working and hustling in the streets (it was enough to buy a new house!) and left Jackson for the DMV.

CHAPTER 5

CULTURE SHOCK

I slept on Uncle D's couch for a few months to gather my bearings. Uncle D had switched jobs and moved from Jackson to work at Howard University, where he was in a leading faculty position. He lived in Silver Spring, Maryland, a suburb several miles outside of D.C. The location made it a perfect place to start my new life. I had finally made it to the "Chocolate City!"

Parliament came out with a song in 1975 called "Chocolate City," which helped the notoriety a bit, I suppose. It was the first American city where most of the population was Black and Black people were the majority inhabitants for over 50 years. It wasn't quite that way when I got there, but there were still more Black people in various professions than I had ever seen. I'll talk more about that later.

When I first arrived in the D.C. area, in 1999, I didn't know what to expect. Everything was faster paced than Mississippi. The tall buildings and fast-walking people were overwhelming at first. D.C. seemed to be worlds away from my hometown. Sure, Jackson was a city, but not like D.C. Jackson takes a nap at night. The city noise seems to quiet down and traffic is light. Jackson didn't hold a candle to D.C. at night. The entire city lights up and comes out to play. In the Chocolate City, it was "lights, camera, action!" The noise came from every direction – traffic, loud sirens, and hearing conversations through the walls in the middle of the night. I felt safer at home in Mississippi, even with the gangs and drug dealers all around. At least, they went home after midnight. Not in D.C.! *Maybe this wasn't such a good idea*, I thought to myself, for a moment.

I noticed everything about D.C. and compared it to home. I realized after a while that there were more beautiful scenes to behold, if I changed my focus. The University of Maryland, Howard and Georgetown were within minutes of each other. The museums with all the rich history, the neighborhoods, the mix of nationalities and even the monuments were beyond belief. The city's architecture truly captivated me. I marveled at the Washington Monument, the Mall, and the U.S. Capitol building. D.C. is even close to New York City. I was in a whole new world in the nation's capital. The experience was definitely a culture shock.

My uncle pushed me to try different food. I tried all kinds of cuisines – Italian, Ethiopian, Arabian, and even Pakistani – by visiting a new restaurant each week. Chinatown looked like a mini version of Beijing. Once you see the vibrant colors of the Friendship Arch, you know you've stepped into a new area of town. There were so many options for food there, but the Mongolian barbecue at Tony Cheng's is second to none! All of this drew me to D.C. and held me there like a permanent tourist. I loved it. But I couldn't be a tourist forever; I had to get to work.

With Uncle D's help, I was able to start graduate school at Howard in 2000. Growing up, watching my mom work in nursing, I aspired to be a doctor. I started in Biology, then changed to Communications, while working with the USDA. I was influenced quite a bit by my co-workers and started to think maybe the medical field wasn't really for me.

A year later, I became a resident assistant on campus. I changed my major to Master of Public Policy/Public Administration, which required me to complete some pre-requisite classes before beginning my program. I was absolutely enthralled with seeing so many professional, beautiful Black people. They were interesting, successful, and progressive. I was impressed and jealous at the same time. I was motivated to push myself further. I made a good impression with my instructors and my assertiveness paid off. Dr. McCormick pulled me aside one day and said coyly, "I need you to go visit the Ralph Bunche Center."

As I headed to the Center, I wondered why I would need to go to the International Affairs Center. It was named after Ralphe J. Bunche, the former head of the Political Science Department. I had no idea that I would be greeted with an opportunity to represent one of Howard University's international programs. I was selected

for the Coax Foundation Scholarship Award for Academics and Internships. My task was to visit Ethiopia,
working for the American Embassy, to observe and
document their current infrastructure and economy. I eagerly received the immunizations and paperwork for the
trip. I couldn't wait to take it all in over a six-month pe-
riod during the Spring and Summer semesters. But Ethiopia wasn't what I expected.

Portrayed as a suffering Third World country on
every American television show I ever watched, my visit
to Ethiopia shattered that myth. I had imagined vast, arid
landscapes and malnourished children with popped-out
bellies based on what I'd seen in the news about this
North African country. Unlike many other African countries, Ethiopia is the only country that did not experience
colonial rule. Many Ethiopians are proud of this, and
they will happily share it with you should you ask. The
beauty of Ethiopia was overwhelming. Ethiopia is green
and lush, and the children are full of energy and curiosity. The families were warm and welcoming. I didn't feel
like an outsider in Ethiopia, but many miles across the
ocean in Mississippi, I felt ostracized as a Black man.

Though I was there to work, I wanted to know more
about my roots. My curiosity made me wander into the
streets of Addis Ababa, the capital city of Ethiopia, on a
quest for more knowledge. I personally wanted to know
more about King Haile Selassie I, Ethiopia's two-
hundred-twenty-fifth, and last, emperor. He had a fasci-

nating story. The longtime ruler traced his line back to Menelik I, who was the child of King Solomon and the Queen of Sheba. King Solomon from the Bible was one of the most interesting characters I'd heard about in church so this was rich to me! The history of King Selassie I was overwhelming and resounded in my spirit for years to come. It wasn't possible to see all the palaces due to high-security measures, especially the palace in Addis Ababa, but I attempted to see most of it.

It was easy to become friends with many of my brothers and sisters of East African descent, learning more about the culture and experiencing the wildlife. Who could ever forget what it was like to feed the hyenas? It was the first time I'd ever seen a hyena, up-close and personal. What I relished most was experiencing how simple it was to find joy in this world. There were people who had no riches or valuables who lived in tents in the desert and were thrilled to send their children to school. It was inspirational to see the joy on their faces as they served me meals and helped me prepare dishes. I had ample time to explore the country and appreciate its authenticity. I visited many cities within Ethiopia, each one gave me a deeper and richer learning experience than the place before.

My days began with a robust cup of coffee. I indulged in the tastes of Ethiopia and often enjoyed the lovely afternoon treat of a creamy caramel Macchiato, upside down. After work, I explored different restaurants to indulge in authentic cuisines. Every bistro or restaurant served Injera, a soft, sour bread, resembling a pancake. I enjoyed the taste, but it was unique. You either loved Injera or you hated it. Served with many tasty vegetarian stews, Injera is a common meal in Ethiopia. The stews were comprised of flavorful chickpeas and lentils. It was delicious!

The best pizza I've ever eaten was in Ethiopia. It was all about the sauce. I gained weight while visiting Ethiopia. That's how much I enjoyed their food. Sometimes, my supervisor, a white guy named Rick, would invite me over for tea or dinner. He lived across the street from my house with his family. The variety of spices and seasonings made my taste buds sing. They were very hospitable and generous to me.

Since I was eating well, I wanted other people to eat well. I established personal relationships with many Ethiopian businesses, which enabled me to give back to the community while I was there. As an Alpha Phi Alpha frat, I felt obligated to do this. I would order food and treats from local catering companies and organize a way to give it away to residents. It was fulfilling, at least, until I became deathly ill from eating some kind of green vegetables. I called Godmom and she prayed with me. Of course, I survived, but I was extremely careful after that.

I lodged in a home where other ambassadors visited when they came to Ethiopia. The estate-style home was massive, gated, and elaborately decorated. Because of pockets of civil unrest, I always traveled with a body-guard. Guards were constantly watching over the house. The bodyguard who monitored my house would bring his son to work and I would help him with his schoolwork and tell him about America when I arrived home from the Embassy.

One of the diplomats was Ambassador Jerome Stapleton. He was a tall, slim man with a warm smile. Ambassador Stapleton was the United States Assistant Secretary of State for African Affairs. He took me under his wing and showed me the personal side of being an ambassador and a public figure. He served as the Ambassador to Guinea and Ethiopia and provided a wealth of information that I was keen to absorb. Working abroad and traveling with Rhode Scholars made me feel like I had finally made it. The skinny kid from Mississippi was working in Ethiopia and providing value to others.

Work was always at high alert. I had only gotten there a month after the students, and the local army had a shootout on the campus of Addis Ababa University. I was responsible for the country report. Gathering information about the country's Gross National Product and economics was my assignment. It was a challenging project, but not because of the work itself. This was the first time I experienced being one of the only African Americans that many locals had ever seen. I felt like most people had already made up their minds about who I was and what I could do for them. No one seemed interested in knowing Cobby.

That all changed when I visited two cities, Dire Dawa and Harar, with my friend, Angelica. I had only known Angelica for about a month; however, she and I became close during her stay in Addis Ababa. I didn't know much about Africa during that time, only what they taught us in school. So, my journey was overwhelming and filled with excitement. Angelica, who was White, was best friends with Carla, a Rhode Scholar and student at Princeton. Carla was one of the nicest and smartest people I'd ever met. The three of us took a two-week vacation and shared a tiny one-bedroom tin house during our adventures.

It was a little awkward because we had to share such a small space. We would shower and change clothes in front of each other as though we'd known each other for years. We had no choice and laughed about it. It was a culture shock for me being in such a strange land and being amongst two American strangers. Here were two Caucasian women showing the Black man around Africa. The irony dumbfounded me!

Angelica and her friends had introduced me to the locals within the village. To many, I was the first African American they had ever seen. They could barely speak English, but they could share what they felt. That they were happy to see me and not moved by worldly, media-driven perceptions of Black people. I strangely felt enlivened.

We spent a week in both cities, Dire Dawa and Harar, touring the local sites. Harar was particularly interesting because it has a centuries-old defensive wall with several enormous gates surrounding the entire city. It is considered a holy city with countless mosques and places of worship. It reminded me of the city of Jericho in the Bible.

Among the holy sites, Ethiopia was undergoing a notable industrial revolution. Business buildings and office parks were springing up across the country. I wrote about the industrial improvements I witnessed firsthand in my country report. It was a wonderful internship. One that would stay with me forever.

Before I left Ethiopia, I felt like things were finally falling into place in my life, but several days before my departure from the lovely country, I felt strange. I had an awful sinking feeling in my stomach. My grandmother always taught me to trust in two things: my gut and God. I knew something wasn't right. I contacted Godmom and told her I was heading home from Ethiopia earlier than expected. She sounded happy to have me returning home. I told her that something just didn't feel right. "Just pray, baby," she suggested. During the ten-hour flight back to the states, I wrestled with an uncomfortable feeling.

I arrived back in D.C. on the morning of September 11, 2001. The world knows what happened that day. My colleague lost a family member and it devastated our entire team. We weren't allowed to talk about the situation, but it affected a lot of people, even me. My uneasy feeling didn't shake with the events of 9-11. I called Godmom and told her I was coming home. I had my mind made up. I was going straight to Godmom's house to put my fears to rest. I arrived at Jackson International Airport and Godmom picked me up. She told me we had to take care of a few things before we headed home.

During the ride, her phone rang. I listened to the details she repeated in a high-pitched tone I didn't recognize, and my heart instantly dropped.

"Have you called 911?" Tears flowed down her cheeks. "Okay, I'm on my way there," she urged as she ended the call and faced me.

"That was Jimmy from the Pager shop. He said Cody has been shot," she cried.

She repeated a prayer under her breath for the duration of the ride. With her foot pressed heavily against the gas pedal, she floored it to the shop.

Suddenly, a feeling of deep despair hit me, and I burst into tears. "He's gone!" I screamed.

She shook her head in denial. "Don't say that, Cobby. Don't say that," she pleaded, but I could tell by the look on her face she already knew the truth.

Lost in our thoughts, the car was eerily silent as we drove to the shopping center where the pager shop was located. It was where I had worked with my family for years. We pulled up to a swarm of emergency workers rushing in and out of the shop in a hurry. The deep aching within my spirit wouldn't let up. I knew what it was telling me. As we walked inside the shop, we faced four, shell-shocked employees. They looked like they had experienced a terrible scene.

It turned out that the shooter came to Cody's autobody shop and shot Cody twice in the head. He tried to shoot the other employees, but his gun jammed. It traumatized everyone, and all I could think about was the jammed gun that prevented my demise in senior high school.

"What happened, Jimmy? Where is he?" Godmom questioned.

Jimmy shook his head sadly. "The emergency workers already took him to the hospital about two minutes ago." Tears were falling down his cheeks. Jimmy Lee was a tall, slender guy, with a warm smile and a big heart. He worked in the pager shop for several years and became a member of the family.

We stared at the large bloodstain on the cement, saying a hopeful prayer that Cody would survive this. I watched as Godmom stood absently in the middle of the shop then I sprang into action.

"Ma, I got all of this. You go be with Dad," I urged, as she seemed to shake herself from the spell. She nodded her agreement and walked out of the shop toward her car and drove to the hospital to be with Cody while I managed the shop. I made sure the business ran smoothly while she tended to Cody. Although I felt hopeless, I also managed to ensure no one took advantage of the current tragedy and used it as an opportunity to steal.

Godmom called from the hospital. When I answered the phone, her voice croaked out in barely a whisper, "He's gone," she said, and burst into tears.

My life changed in that very second. Losing my godfather that way hurt me to the depths of my soul. Cody wasn't about the violence. He was a mentor, a good man. He was the father I so desperately needed.

I recalled my grandmother's wise words, "People can come into your life for a reason, a season, or a lifetime." Cody came into my life for a reason. He believed in me and taught me I could be a better man than what my stepfather showed me. His murder was a devastating loss for the entire family and the community.

I returned to D.C. and tried my best to pick up the pieces of my life. Cody deserved better than what he got. He was the man who taught me how to be thoughtful about my life choices. He showed me how to live my life by example. I struggled with my own sadness and my despondency for Godmom, who had to move on without the love of her life.

A few weeks later, back in D.C., work, again, became my everything. I dedicated my life to my career. My goal was to stay as busy as possible and tried to push the tragic circumstances behind me. I attempted to manage my grief over my godfather's loss by focusing on the good times and everything he taught me. But I desperately wanted to know who murdered him. Finally, we learned that authorities had apprehended the killer.

A mentally disturbed young man took my godfather away from the family who loved him dearly. The young man had gotten it in his head that my godfather was responsible for the death of his family members. Someone murdered two people in his family, and he felt the need to take his frustrations out on my godfather. The disturbed lad killed Cody to avenge the murder of his relatives.

Murder is an extreme solution for some of the most trivial reasons. In Jackson, I knew it to be normal, but the attempt on me and the execution of Cody was too much to comprehend. Young kids shooting and killing people in broad daylight because they can't silence the voices in their head I saw as an effect of disadvantages in a community. It was a tragic loss all the way around. My family changed after we lost him. I changed.

CHAPTER 6

A NEW JOURNEY

"Just pray, baby," Godmom's words kept ringing in my head. I knew how to pray some prayers, but I was lost about how to pray about the loss of my godfather. There were days when I didn't know up from down. I missed him terribly and I wanted answers to questions I couldn't articulate well enough to ask anyone.

Upon my return to D.C., I dove back into work. It's funny when I think about it now, but the USDA wasn't all stuffy and boring in D.C. I recall within my first three weeks being there, my manager, Billy, introduced me to a lot of people, but I never expected to meet President Bill Clinton. It was a Tuesday when Billy got the call. He rushed over to me, frantically, saying, "We have to get to the other side of the White Building now!" I was wearing a navy suit, white shirt, and tie. At least, I was dressed appropriately!

President Clinton gave a short speech welcoming all the new hires in his administration. Then, he greeted us individually. He gave me a firm handshake. I didn't say a word. I didn't know what to say! I was fresh off the plane from "M-I-crooked letter-crooked letter-I-crooked letter-crooked letter-I-humpback-humpback-I!" It's kind of funny that Billy introduced me to Bill. I digress. I thanked Billy for rushing me over there. It was his first introduction as well. You never knew who you would meet in D.C.

I will never forget two men I met at the agency, Mr. W and Mr. C. They were international travelers for the USDA. I admired everything about these two charismatic Black men from their suits and ties, right down to their shoes. They carried themselves with class and dignity. Every time I saw them, they were in teacher mode with me. They taught me how to carry myself as a professional Black man. It was surprising for me to learn different ways to tie my tie. Oh, and the stories they told about how chocolate in Switzerland was better than chocolate from the Netherlands made me want to travel more!

As I was entering my fifth year at the USDA, I worked as a chauffeur on the weekends to drive important people around. It would take some people a lifetime to meet as many celebrities as I had. I recall driving Boys II Men one evening to their hotel. They were speaking about the logistics of their shows, who was performing and in what order. They were all about business! I wasn't allowed to say anything. It was a part of the job. They were in their zone though. Just being in their presence was an honor. I had watched them my entire life.

On another occasion, I drove Steve Harvey and his crew to the WHUR 96.3 FM radio station. We later went to dinner and he randomly asked me what I was up to and what my plans were for my life. I told him I was running for Congress someday, and he said, "Go for it, man! I like to hear that." I beamed while he continued talking. "Yeah, man, follow your heart. You're young. What do you have to lose?"

In the back of my mind, I remembered all the trials and tribulations I'd gone through in Mississippi and even at Howard. Who would have ever thought I would sit across from Steve Harvey, having dinner and talking politics? This was another treasured moment in my life. There were times I felt like a celebrity and times when my close friends, relatives and students heard about these moments and dismissed my enthusiasm. It was disappointing, but I couldn't let their words get me down too much. I had to get on with doing me. That's a hard lesson to learn and sometimes you must learn it repeatedly.

With my day job, I took the opportunity to transfer to another department within the USDA as a Public Affairs Specialist with the Agricultural Marketing Services. The supervisor was a Black woman. I thought I could learn a lot from her and that it would be a wonderful experience, but it wasn't. Things went awry too quickly and we seemed to quarrel every day. It went downhill from there. It was a lot of pressure on both of us. Before there was any unnecessary escalation, I left. I was devastated. I worked hard to avoid any trouble, not just with Black women, but with anyone. Simply because the trauma of not being able to control what's around you is numbing.

During that time, I also worked part-time at two hotels in D.C., as a night auditor. I didn't even know who
managed the hotel until several months had passed. Believe it or not, it was another Black woman. After we
met, I started to wonder if it was them or me? Now, I'm
not a conspiracy theorist nor do I want to ever stereotype
a particular group. I'm just speaking from my experience. My experience there wasn't all bad though. From
my mentors, I learned three valuable lessons:

Always stay busy, even if there's nothing going on
in the office. Find a way to be productive.

Always dress appropriately for every occasion. Men
look you up and down to judge how they will speak to
you. They will either treat you as a superior, an equal or
a subordinate.

Pay close attention to your etiquette when you're
around people of importance and those who want to in-
vest in you. Always show respect. You never know when
you'll be faced with those individuals again.

In any case, I had to get out of the USDA fast. I left
that job, looked for something more suitable, and focused
more on school. You wouldn't believe I was the same
guy who didn't want to attend college at all. If my grandmother could have seen me then, it would've amazed her.
She told me to go all the way and I did. She would have
been proud to see that I didn't spend all my hard-earned
money from Jackson sight-seeing in the DMV.

I house-hunted on days I wasn't working or going to school. My best friend, Calvin, from Alabama, was in the area and, one day, I visited his home in D.C. There was a condo for sale near him and I inquired about it. It was a one-bedroom condo in a Federal-style building facing Rhode Island Avenue, in Ward five, the largest Ward in D.C. From the small closet that I let California Closets® redesign, to the mini hallway, I treasured my little hotel-like home. And, I had the best housewarming party. My friends from JSU, Ethan and Dalton, came to D.C. to study law and joined my party along with Calvin and a few others. I felt so free that night. Probably a little too free. After all, I had to get to church the next morning.

My faith has always been and still is paramount in my life. I attended random churches in the area and the Andrew Rankin Memorial Chapel on campus. I never missed Sunday services, but I was still walking around angry, but also kind of empty and lost. In the summer of 2005, I decided to visit a church that was just down the street from my condo. The day I walked into New Hope changed the trajectory of my life.

When the Co-Pastor arose to speak, her words capti-vated my soul. Now, this Black woman's unwavering faith and wisdom compelled me to listen. She touched my heart. Co-Pastor had a lovely spirit, which spoke di-rectly to me. I was feeling out of place in this world, I had no church home, and I was missing my mother. She reminded me of home and that motherly love. I surrendered and accepted my purpose that day.

Becoming Pentecostal was quite different than my roots at Mississippi Baptist Church. I read the Bible much more and went in depth with the scriptures. I witnessed the power of the Holy Spirit moving all through the sanctuary. There were people running, dancing, and speaking in tongues. I didn't speak in tongues, but I surely felt the Spirit of God in that house. The music was, by far, the best I've ever heard. The "War Cry" is my favorite. It's the melody the whole church sings in unity. We praised God in that place! And, when the word was good, congregants would throw money at the preacher. You know people don't just throw money for no reason at nobody! I was captivated.

The Co-Pastor reminded me of Mom. Reflecting on my issues with women in leadership, I often wondered if they were going through something or if it was something I did. I couldn't put my finger on why I seemed to keep clashing with them, but with Co-Pastor, it just felt different. At church, she was all about business and ministry. Her voice was commanding. She clarified things in bible class that I'd wondered about for years. As I got to know her more personally, I found her to be sweet, genuine, and full of wisdom. Motherly love wasn't something I was used to with Mom working all the time. Co-Pastor's demonstration of love and compassion made me feel like I was in a new land.

Eventually, I began biblical studies at New Hope's

Bible Institute to earn a Biblical Certification in 2007. It reminded me of my college courses and was much more disciplined than bible study at the Baptist church in Mississippi. I also worked for over five years under the bishop's tutelage. It was an honor to serve Bishop and Co-Pastor, who have a lovely family. They took me in and I, immediately, felt like family. I still feel that way. Flashbacks to my childhood while I was with the bishop's family would happen often. It reminded me of the good times shared with my siblings, my mom and stepfather (without the arguing and cussing from my stepfather, that is). Then, there were times I was told everything was going to be all right when Mom was working hard to keep food on the table. When the flashbacks hit me, like nightmares in the daytime, I learned how to hit back with scripture and prayer. The bishop's family taught me how to really pray and have a conversation with God about every desire while being grateful for what you already have and what He's already done. It was a healing experience.

I functioned in many capacities at the church. One of my favorite roles was being a faithful member of the usher board. Eventually, I obtained a position at the church serving as an Adjutant to the Senior Bishop. This experience changed my way of thinking, my feelings and how I approached relationships. Serving a man of God wasn't as easy as working for a manager or supervisor within the government. This church serves the people.

I'm proud to say I am a member of this great church and found a new place called "home."

I took the bishop's grandson to school and even helped him with his homework. Often Bishop's armor bearers would share ideas, insight, and wisdom with one another. As the administrative assistant to the bishop, I participated in those discussions. I never expected to have the privilege to travel abroad with him. Pure joy filled my heart when I had the opportunity to pull out my passport again.

Greater New Hope International Ministries had multiple churches in various countries throughout the world. Each year, when these churches held celebrations, the bishop and his family would also attend. As part of the staff, I would travel to these countries with them. I traveled to London with the bishop. London is such a historic and beautiful place that I spent a great deal just taking in the sights. It had been years since I visited London with my school and now, here I was, returning as the armor bearer for the bishop. Now, food was another story. Cold bread, soup, fish and chips, biscuits, and pastries... We ate at exceptionally fine restaurants, but I had more tea and crumpets than I ever care to eat again!

We visited a church just outside of London. The building was massive and, to my surprise, packed with people of color. The bishop spoke at the church service, ushering in a spirit of praise within the large brick and mortar building. He then asked me to lead a prayer. Me!

It was the greatest seal of approval I had ever received. This meant that he trusted me! I can't explain the feeling I had the moment I spoke to the congregation. I stood in front of the three-hundred-plus-member congregation and prayed as if it were only God and me. When I finished, the sanctuary erupted in praise. It was truly a beautiful moment in my life.

We then traveled to Trinidad and Tobago in 2005, a beautiful Caribbean country with stunning beaches and lots of tourists. I loved the land, but the powerful experience was witnessing the glory of God in the lives of so many people. Traveling with the church opened my eyes wider to the world. I enjoyed myself in those days. I was still very magnetized by women and they were attracted to me.

So, yeah, I dated a lot in church. Admittedly, so much that I almost got kicked out! This was my fault and no one else's, so I won't dwell on that part. Perfection is not a word I'd use to describe my history, but I learned a great deal. For one thing, while it's alright to seek relationships, limiting how many you have at a time and how deep they get might save your ass! It was time to simmer down and lay low. As graduate school was wrapping up, a new opportunity presented itself with the Office of Personnel Management as a Strategic Human Resource Specialist. The two years provided immense education on government laws and regulations. At that point, I wasn't sure where my career would take me next, but the familiarity of policies eventually proved to be useful.

I concentrated on learning as much as I could. Training events and conferences were my go-to places to acquire more skills. The hustler in me made me want to work as many different jobs as I could. I believe that learning new things kept your brain fresh and your mind eager for more. Fast-paced Washington, D.C. kept me on my toes. I met a lot of movers and shakers in the political arena, and, thankfully, those contacts opened the door for me to work on two major political campaigns.

Through an association with dear friends, I learned that mayoral candidate, Adonis Fields, was seeking help with his campaign. Mr. Fields was a young city council member from Ward 4, which was Uptown in Northwest D.C., near Silver Spring, MD, where I used to live. I was determined to prove that I was the man for the job. The more I became involved with his campaign, the more intrigued I became with politics, but it was a demanding schedule. I spent weeks knocking on doors and meeting the people in the neighborhoods. Councilman Fields had an aggressive plan for going door-to-door and it worked for him as he won his re-election and eventually became the Mayor of D.C.

It was astounding how many D.C. political figures came out of Ward 4. Councilman Fields' campaign strategy afforded me the opportunity to see the variety of people who lived in Ward 4. I might describe the area as if there were pockets of different ways of life. There were families who had two-story homes and then, right across the street, homeless people in the park. Some couldn't care less if you were bringing them good news or bad. While there were others who showed genuine interest in what you had to say.

I recall a woman named Mary who was an older, white woman with gray hair. After speaking with Mary, she emailed and called me all the time asking for updates on events. The sound of her voice reminded me of my grandmother. She was such a nice lady. Mary didn't leave me with any deep, philosophical thoughts, but she did enlighten me on how people would react to my introduction of the councilman's candidacy.

"Now, I'll tell you who will agree with you and who won't," she said, calmly. I laughed, respectfully. She was very diplomatic with her responses and always cordial.

Being in the community helped me learn how to talk to people and translate their needs into sound bites for the campaign, which would eventually become components of policies. Ultimately, I became a campaign organizer and I found great joy in this new vocation. I spent several months to a year being a part of this campaign trail. It was the first time I thought, "This experience is worth more than the pay!" I never thought that before. "I must have found my niche!" Suddenly, I had this overwhelming, familiar feeling. It reminded me of two moments: one from my childhood and one from college. I closed my eyes and envisioned the tall, light-skinned man in a gray suit from Mississippi. Back then, even though I wanted to be a doctor, his striking image was mesmeric. The other moment I recalled was from my freshman year at JSU when I won the election for Mr. Freshman. The feeling I had winning that election was surreal. I don't know if this moment of recollection was an epiphany, but I felt compelled to explore the political arena even more.

My on-the-job lessons in fundraiser planning, polling, getting out the vote, and maintaining contact with the public led me to finesse this campaign job into a full-on career and I enjoyed it. The inner workings of political parties were beguiling. You didn't just learn from the candidate you supported, but in that environment, you learned from all types of experts from project managers to financial wizards.

Every campaign needs investors to operate properly and successfully. I didn't know where that money came from at first. I discovered that many politicians run campaigns solely off the funds of special interests and investor groups. It became fully apparent to me that those groups had to know what you were going to do for them before they invested in a candidate. I suppose the real shock was that some candidates only had the interests of their big supporters in mind, not the public.

This befuddled me as I noticed that there weren't many people in politics who looked like me or came from neighborhoods like mine. I soon realized that proper representation in D.C. was a social imperative. But what could I do about it? I wondered, silently, as I continued absorbing knowledge from the activities around me. It appeared that the rich guy wanted to get richer, so he invested in the political candidate to create policies to increase his wealth. Other investors were just trying to protect what money they had, so they supported political candidates who restrict certain tax increases and liabilities.

I began to wonder, if special interest groups and investors only finance campaigns to gain power or money, who were the people in D.C. trying to make a difference for my homies in Jackson? I had to find the answer to questions like this because I was starting to feel as if there was never an absolute noble motive behind investing in politics. I was a novice, but there was no better place to learn than on Capitol Hill.

Capitol Hill is a crazy place. While walking the halls, I found myself comparing the experience with Congress to the drug game in Jackson. Senators, like drug dealers, threw massive parties with people they rocked with. In various corners, in different buildings, they were trading papers and secrets like crack and hush money. Somebody was responsible for counting that money, but the person responsible for counting the money wasn't even getting 1% of what they were adding up.

Political parties behaved like distributors or cartels. I

was there reading, studying, and watching the policies being implemented within the United States. I knew who wrote the deal, who cut the deal and who the winners and losers were from the deal. It was wild, but I had to find a way to build relationships and make mental notes of my observations. I didn't realize I was preparing for my own new journey in politics. I knew the world wanted to put limitations on the Black community, but it didn't stop me from engaging in various conversations and recognizing that I could be more of a participant in this process than an eager observer.

I had immersed myself into the political business of Washington and, in due course, I learned three valuable lessons:

(1) Policymaking is never final. If a new administration comes on board, any policy could change.

(2) Politicians are always switching parties. This makes policy making difficult. Any party with lack of membership participation could lose a vote to pass legislation.

(3) Lobbyists tend to control many of the outcomes of policy making.

Every day, after my introduction to politics, I took a moment to imagine myself running my own campaign. As with many other areas in my life, it started with a thought. Once I formulated a thought about something, I wanted to see it through to the end. I discovered that thoughts could plant the seed of hope, and all I must do is nurture it to the point of success. It took me burning a couple of bridges to learn that networking was more about farming than it was about hunting. You plant the seeds, water them, care for them, and watch your plants grow. That's how things worked for me. When you treat people like game you have to hunt, you'll find yourself being hunted. Eventually, I planted the right seeds and nurtured relationships that were important for my growth and career.

I wished Cody could see me. I didn't think I would survive without his daily guidance. A very immature and selfish young man showed up to D.C. in the beginning. I didn't take all my relationships seriously. I was comfortable treating people I encountered as ships passing during the night. Over time, it became important to care more about other people's predicaments.

It's necessary to respect all walks of life and begin to value others' perspectives. I'm not afraid of commitment in personal or professional relationships like I was when I stuffed all my savings in the trunk of my Ford and fled from Jackson. There were still uneasy feelings when I thought about the loss of Cody in my life, but I was grateful for the nuggets gleaned from the new people who poured into me because I certainly needed to heal from the despicable words I grew up hearing.

CHAPTER 7

FIGHTING VICIOUS WORDS AND MAKING HISTORY

Who wasn't teased as a kid? I had my share of the dozens being played on me. If it wasn't my big nose, it was my big lips. If not the big lips, it was my big ears. It didn't help that my brother and I got our haircuts from random folks in the neighborhood versus a professional barbershop. The hustling barbers didn't specialize in sanitation. Often my brother and I would discover ringworms and other unknown fungi growing on our scalps. This would go on for years until I could afford to go to a professional barber. Never again would a miserable soul from my family tell me I had to get a haircut by the person of their choice. To this day, I prioritize having a decent haircut and looking presentable. That's why I always had a fresh haircut if I was in America, Central America, Europe, Africa, or Asia.

The more money I made, the better clothes I would purchase, too. I bought designer suits and other attire with high-end labels. I was intentional about looking good from the haircut down to my shoes and socks. I didn't want to look like that ungroomed child ever again.

My stepfather used to make us feel deplorable most days. "You will never be shit in life," he would say.

"You ain't never gonna be nothing!" How do you overcome words like that? Those vicious words made my
brother and I feel like outcasts! They stuck in my head
and even to my very soul. I guess you could say I
thought perfecting my outward appearance as a man
would heal the little boy inside.

Outwardly, my life was wonderful, but internally I
was struggling with things that tried to become a stronghold over my spirit. Between the words of my stepfather
haunting me and the loss of my godfather, I was in a bad
place. Anger and frustration ruled my thoughts. I spent a
lot of time cursing folks out. My grandmother used to
say, "If you have nothing nice to say to anyone, then
don't say it at all." God bless her soul! I heard her voice
one day and, for the first time in a long time, I looked in
the mirror and I didn't like what I saw.

The reflection was the angry, hurt, and abused young
kid. All I could see was the younger version of Cobby
that liked to use my fists to communicate instead of my
words. The anger in my spirit made me restless and sad.

During my childhood years in Canton, my next-door
neighbor, Dave, was a Jehovah's Witness. He was the
kindest guy I knew during that time. He invited me to
church often, and I enjoyed the experience. There was a
great feeling of togetherness and warmth that drew me
in. Of course, my grandmother attended a Baptist church
and I spent a lot of time with her there. I spent most of
my life in different churches, experiencing unique ways

to praise and give thanks. Proverbs 22:6 says, "Train up a child in the way he should go, and when he is old, he will not depart from it." I genuinely believe this scripture plays out in everyday life. With all of my different religious experiences, I needed to strengthen my foundation before I made the next big move.

Being in church again in D.C. had given me such a sweet solace. I could finally take a long, hard look at Cobby Williams. I began the journey to find myself and realized I had to do some deep thinking to turn my life around. The journey would require me to be honest with myself about what I wanted in life. Even though it's a difficult task, checking my behavior and putting a stop to the habits interfering with my goals was a necessary task. Sometimes, that's what we must do in life. I found myself at that crossroads between my comfortable old life and the inner calm I sought.

I felt my grandmother's spirit guiding me back to that place of comfortability. Her voice guided me back to the house of the Lord. I was distressed, depressed, and feeling hopeless. When I backslid away from the church, I was a Baptist. I returned to the church but not to the same reformation. I became Pentecostal, and my entire being transformed right before me. I was ready for the next big thing.

Do you remember the profound moments in your life, those moments when you receive confirmation for your dreams or plans? One of my moments came on an afternoon when I was leaving my office. I stepped through the large office doors and into the bright sunshine. I paused for a moment, allowing the sun to warm my face as I considered my next move.

I was twenty-nine years old and had successfully navigated graduate school at Howard University. My time at Howard taught me more than I could have ever imagined. I learned that: 1) education was for those who want it; 2) opportunities are for those who seek them; and 3) helping someone along the way is a worthwhile investment.

After everything I had been through, I earned my master's degree from a prestigious university. I should have felt more accomplished, but I felt like something was missing. By this time, I had been working within the federal government for years. As I stood outside of the building, a little girl was walking up the steps with her mother. She turned to face me and smiled. Her blue eyes were wide with wonder as she asked, "Are you a congressman?" I smiled at her and shook my head in response.

Several hours later, that little girl's words plagued my thoughts for the entire weekend. I woke up Monday morning with a renewed mind and a definitive plan for my next move. That moment solidified my decision to run for office.

Godmom always referred to me as the consummate politician because I could make a friend out of anyone by talking to them. I always wanted to run for office and become a politician. Several things inspired me, but nothing like meeting that tall, Black congressman when I was in fourth grade. I felt like he passed the torch to me when I met him the first time. Even though I was incredibly young, the moment stuck with me for many years and this moment took me right back to the 9-year-old me.

In Jackson, I didn't see many politicians or famous people, so that meeting was more than just a chance conversation, it was my first indicator of things to come. I spent nearly ten years within various federal agencies, meeting and working with different politicians and community advocates. I believed I had gained enough experience to begin a campaign and what better place to make an impact than in the place where I grew up?

As someone growing up in crime and poverty-stricken areas, I had a front-row seat to hopelessness. I was all too familiar with what was causing the suffering in my communities. I wanted to uplift them and provide a reason to be hopeful that somebody cared and improvements could be achieved in their neighborhoods.

After mulling over my decision for a few days, I called Godmom. Thrilled with my decision, she wanted me to move back to her house and run for Congress in Jackson, Mississippi. I had other plans, though. I wanted to run in the city where I was born. I believed it was the right thing to do. So, I packed up my condo in Northeast,

D.C., and moved back home to Canton, Mississippi, to make history.

I had to rent out my property so I could move to Mississippi. I decided that I was going to move into my grandma's house. It was the perfect residence for a county seat. The neighborhood was familiar and several people who I knew still lived there. The days leading up to my first night back in my hometown were nerve-wracking and thrilling at the same time. My first night was in a hotel where I made plans to start my campaign journey in the morning. That was short-lived exhilaration as I awakened to the news that my grandma's house caught on fire.

I was devastated. How could this have happened? I was literally just about to get started with what I thought was the greatest time of my life. After the fire was extinguished and the arson investigators finished their exploration, they told me someone left a candle burning inside. This loss left a gaping hole in my heart. I was counting on staying at my grandmother's house because I knew she believed in me. It killed my spirit for quite some time.

That night in the hotel became the first of several months in the same place. What would that look like in the news? *Headline: New Congressional Candidate Lives in Hotel.* Those were very emotional days. It was a hindrance that nearly stopped me from running for the county seat. Eventually, I sucked it up and hit the campaign trail anyway. I stayed in the hotel until I could secure a place in downtown Canton. We found a small place downtown for the campaign headquarters. I set up various meetings with the mayor, councilpersons, and other city officials and got to work.

God always had an angel looking out for me. In every new endeavor, travel opportunity, or experience, there has been someone to help me along the way. Politics was no exception. I had a mentor who showed me a lot about campaigns that I didn't know. I learned a lot from my frat brother. This guy, John, took me under his wing and showed me the ropes. He helped me set up panels where community members could tell me what they needed and wanted. Although I worked on several large campaigns in D.C., I didn't know the full extent of running one.

The truth is, you don't know what it takes to manage a campaign until you run your own. It's a personal experience that's unlike any other. You see things completely differently, but the excitement of running for office was intoxicating. I had a good team working with me, and I felt a high level of respect from all of them. I needed that.

I tried to stay two steps ahead of trouble and to listen to people letting them know they had my ear. It was a struggle to get to know the people around the county. I found my approach wasn't quite working. My goal was to work for the people; to bring tax dollars to the area and to work across the aisles on positive legislation. Congresspersons do have power and influence. "Of course, I can effect change," I thought to myself daily. I started eagerly sharing my ideas about how our city and county could be better but kept hitting a wall. It was hard to change their thought process. Some people perceived me as a guy who thought he was better than other folks.

I returned to Mississippi expecting people to welcome me with open arms, especially those who had the same skin color as mine. Man was I surprised! One of my first meetings was with a representative from the Black Republicans Group in Canton. I sat across from an impeccably dressed older gentleman with a graying mustache and beard. He smiled at me as he measured his words carefully.

"We think you have bitten off more than you can chew. I know you are ambitious, but don't you think it would fare better for you if you ran for City Council or the School Board, first?"

I stared at him in complete shock as he continued to explain that my plans would surely fail.

"You can't help these people. They don't understand your way of thinking," he surmised.

I said nothing. I learned that if you let people talk long enough, they will tell you everything you need to know about their character.

This brother looked like he could be my kin, but I felt like his goal was to discourage me from running. He spent forty minutes of our meeting speaking ill about the "country Negroes" in his district.

"They are going to listen to you speak, sounding like you're from D.C. and they will tune you right out," he prophesied. He spoke so negatively about Black people that I had to question if he wasn't a White man dressed in blackface.

Now, there was some truth to the things he stated. Madison County is a small municipality with a lot of history and heart. The Black population in Madison County was reeling from police policies, which resulted in arresting a substantial part of the population. Police arrested Black residents five times more than Whites. A place where less than half of the 100,000 residents hold a bachelor's degree, Madison County was as rural as it could get. Still, I felt in my heart he spoke from a place of fear. When people are afraid to do things themselves, they try to discourage others. Fear is nothing more than a virus. It is contagious if you allow yourself to be susceptible to it. I couldn't let fear infect me.

I ended that meeting feeling more determined to win the seat. I wanted to give the minority community a voice, and I didn't want the only voice to be from people who still referred to their constituents as "poor, country Negroes." I wish this was my only time experiencing racist views from people who shared the same ethnicity, but it wasn't.

While walking up and down the streets, knocking on

doors and handing out campaign literature, I noticed some of the voting constituents wouldn't even look me in the eye. As we canvassed neighborhoods some people even threatened to call the police if I stepped one foot on their property. People sat on their porches and as we approached them, they abruptly stood and marched inside their homes. I endured a great deal of animosity and racism from different people, and I, admittedly, wasn't prepared for the comportment from the Black community. Nevertheless, I was undeterred.

I became the youngest candidate, Black or White, to run for Congress in Mississippi. I ran against a long-standing incumbent in the 2012 Congressional Primaries as an Independent candidate. He had eighteen years of service under his belt while I was a thirty-five-year-old, wide-eyed, eager candidate. Although I've been a democratic voter my entire adult life, I had to change my party affiliation to an independent to be placed on the ballot.

The eighteen-year veteran incumbent had huge finances, including personal wealth, aggressive wealthy donors, and special interest groups in his corner. I knew this, but still felt confident enough within myself to run against him. This wasn't the first time I had come up against adversity, and I was sure it would not be the last. This was, however, the first time I realized how treacherous the political arena truly was for someone "green" to the truth. This candidacy taught me so much about people and the way they think. It also taught me that no one is who he or she appears to be, and that is the absolute truth.

CHAPTER 8

BOUNCING BACK

Returning to Mississippi was a sobering process for me. The time I spent in various places made my return impactful. I knew I hailed from one of the poorest states in the country, but I didn't realize the extent of the economic depression. Driving within the city limits, I saw abandoned homes, dilapidated structures where people still lived, and homelessness. It was depressing to see the level of hopelessness in the state. It hurt to see my people living as if they knew nothing of the advancement of Black people. I felt a sense of purpose when I returned to Madison County.

Sure, the racism was a whole other animal, but experiencing judgment from those who looked like me was a large pill to swallow. While racism existed in D.C., it wasn't nearly as upfront and in-your-face like in Mississippi. I wanted to energize the Black citizens and prepare them to use their voices through voting to change our community. Warrantless home searches, police brutality, and a sluggish education system were my main political points.

This campaign was symbolic to me, as 2012 was the beginning of President Obama's last term. I felt honored to run for Congress. He campaigned on the message of change. I wanted change, too, and his message was a symbol of hope for me that I could follow. So many things were changing, while so much remained the same. They called me called the "young gun" because I was running against a seasoned politician. They said I was jumping the line. We were taught to wait for your turn, but I was going against that model. It seemed everything I learned in college flew out of the window.

Back in Mississippi, I was once again inside the "belly of the beast," kicking up dust. Jackson is the central part of Mississippi and the streets were still broken. Houses were still abandoned. It appeared that tax dollars weren't being invested into the neighborhoods. The district still seemed poor. It looked the same as it did when I was a little kid. The books I read didn't teach about suffering, grassroots organizing, and real people issues in politics. Several people in the community weren't on my side. I felt a lot of pressure to give up. This was a different kind of fight.

I felt the spirit of the slavery ancestors on my back. All these years of fighting physically, mentally, and emotionally and the atmosphere felt like we were at a standstill. From the economics side of things, I knew we could do better. When I introduced myself as the incumbent's opponent, people constantly asked me, "Why are you running against him?" It was as if they were afraid and that I should be afraid, too, but I believed we had the strength of the ancestors on our side. We are their great-grandchildren's children. Somebody had to believe we can have better and we deserve better.

I wanted a better infrastructure, funding to bring about employment, and to implement programs to decrease the growing population of prisoners. While I had a great deal of respect for the incumbent, overall, I wanted to bring a new energy and unity within the state. I had to try and, hopefully, this would inspire someone else who would come behind me.

Godmom's words replayed in my head. She told me I had always been a politician. Skills that I gained from years of networking in college and working in federal agencies prepared me to tackle the hurdle before me. It made me happy to see her vision come to life. I held scholarship drives and neighborhood events to reach out to the community. The things I wanted to do pumped energy and fervor into the hearts of some of the constituents.

I needed to secure a job or two to keep me sustained during the campaign. I wanted to be sure I could still make it in Mississippi without touching my savings account. I applied to become a night auditor at one of the local hotels since I had done that successfully in D.C. I also applied for a position in the local school district hoping to become a substitute teacher. The pay was steady and the opportunity to influence children positively was electrifying.

On the campaign trail, I learned how to reach people

from various socioeconomic backgrounds and invigorate their need to be a part of something big. Since I was a talker, I would strike up a conversation with just about anyone, anywhere. I would stop people at the gas station, the grocery store and even the car wash to ask them about what they thought the issues the community was facing. I fully immersed myself in all things political, so I could establish a firm foundation in the county. In truth, I didn't realize the full enormity of what I planned to do, I just jumped into it.

By the time my candidacy became public, my team helped me develop three approaches to the campaign. The first was community events like back-to-school drives, cookouts, and clothing drives. We later added in book scholarships which were granted to graduating high school seniors. The last area was voter registration. Volunteers canvassed neighborhoods and helped register constituents to vote. I enjoyed seeing the community work together toward a common goal. The smiles on family members' faces made me feel like I was doing something positive and on the right track. I was proud of my accomplishments at such an early age. Most of the people who entered the campaign were decades older, which made me more determined to see this adventure through to the end.

Regrettably, I was so focused on my campaign that I didn't see the devil in the details. While canvassing neighborhoods one day, I met someone who would completely alter my life for many years. Melissa was a sweet woman with a warm smile who I was trying to convince to support my campaign. Melissa said she wasn't sure if she could vote. I assumed she was unaware of her voting rights and encouraged her to register anyway with hundreds of others whose information I had also collected. I was unaware that this one act would turn into something so major.

I campaigned and canvassed as hard as I could, but ultimately, I lost to the incumbent by a landslide. I didn't take the loss too hard. I bounced right back. I knew my chances were not the greatest when I began my campaign, but it was all worth it. I learned a new district in Madison County had an opening for the City Council. I couldn't wait to toss my hat in the ring. I didn't stop campaigning. It had become a significant part of my life. I was on a mission for the future, and no one could stop me.

Along with several people that I knew very well, I took the opportunity to run for the City Council. My grade schoolteacher, an elder from the church, along with my first cousin, became my opponents. The race for City Council was a heavily watched competition, and the competition was great for the community because they ultimately ended up with what they needed.

I felt invincible. I was running in my second political campaign in a year. You couldn't tell me I wasn't on the fast track to achieving my goals. I was moving so fast; I couldn't tell there was a deep valley up ahead.

By this time, I learned plenty about canvassing neighborhoods and the importance of hosting events and rallies. My cousin and I defeated the other opponents and made it to the preliminaries. I just knew I had secured my place in the game. That's when it all took a turn for the worse.

It started with a knock on the door.

Melissa came to my house and said, "I think I'm going to get in trouble for registering to vote."

"Don't worry," I pleaded with her in a calm voice, "I'll own up to advising you to fill out the voter registration card." I didn't know what I had gotten myself into.

Melissa began to explain that she was prepared to take full responsibility for everything that happened. Knowledge of the law is absolutely essential for a successful, uninterrupted campaign. I was oblivious to the fact that it was illegal for a convicted felon to cast a ballot. Melissa didn't tell me she was a felon. I think, in the end, she covered her ass because what she did could have landed her in prison for years.

I didn't realize it would be so bad. I unconsciously found myself trying to comfort her almost as if I had intentionally talked her into doing something unlawful. Unbeknownst to me, Melissa had visited my house wired up.

The next thing I knew, the Assistant Attorney General summoned me to his office. Seated at the table with four white men and one Black man, they knew I held no fear. My family in Canton were well known for politicians. I had family members on the school board and my uncle was the first tax collector to go around and pick up payments for taxes. For some reason, I remember that he carried a gun. I suppose it was necessary for carrying enormous amounts of cash. I was all too familiar with that. We were known for our public service. I had a spirit of fulfilling our family destiny so what could interrupt that?

That's when they told me I committed fraud by registering Melissa to vote. They tried to get me to snitch on people who had worked in and around my campaign. I was so green. I had no clue about the shark wading pool where I was sinking. My family supported me the best they could. We were all going through distinct phases in our lives. Some of my siblings were welcoming children, starting their lives over, or blazing a different trail in their lives. They didn't hesitate to let me know they were proud of my accomplishments, but this time, I felt like I was weaved in a tangled web with no support. I denied doing anything wrong, but I didn't know what would happen next.

Then, one day, the shit hit the fan. I was walking my dog and got a call from the Sheriff. "What's going on?" I asked him. He said we needed to talk. I explained I would be available as soon as I finished with the dog. I really just wanted to buy some time to think.

I had a sinking feeling in my gut that the phone call was just the beginning of my worries. There was a warrant out for my arrest, and I had no idea about it. I was contemplating getting on the bus and fleeing back to D.C. I got home from walking the dog, and the sheriff was waiting with handcuffs. My neighbors had to take care of my dog. When they come for you; you cannot prepare for it. That was the scariest time of my life.

When I was younger, my brother, JJ, was super spoiled. One day, I stole a White Sox fitted baseball cap. I thought, "I want some stuff, too!" The manager of the store caught me and, before I knew it, I was in juvenile detention. My family, who made me feel like I was a black sheep – an outcast – was surely talking behind my back. Luckily, I only spent a few hours in detention and I was glad that was it. I didn't want to go to jail then after all I'd done to change my life, I certainly didn't want to go to jail now. Here I was faced with something much more serious.

The court system took no mercy on me. The judge who heard my case was angry. I could feel the tension in the courtroom as he spoke to me through clenched teeth. When the Public Defender informed me of my charges and the possible ramification, I was dumbfounded.

"Five years in jail for the felony charge of voter fraud?!" I yelled. I was devastated.

It was a Friday so, of course, I spent the entire weekend in jail. The seventy-two hours behind metal bars was the worst feeling in my life. I wouldn't wish three days within a Mississippi jail on anyone. It isn't like anything you could ever conceive. To survive, I had to use the mentality that helped me survive the streets of Jackson, Mississippi. I kept to myself as much as possible and didn't offer to share any details about my situation. When other inmates asked my charges, I shrugged and told them the truth. I learned early on that those in jail judged inmates harsher than the public judged them.

Everyone wanted to know what an inmate's charges were so they could determine how to treat them. Some earned a level of respect, while pedophiles and molesters earned a well-deserved ass whooping. Guilty by association was a real thing in jail. I learned early on not to even associate with those convicted of sick sexual abuse crimes.

My nerves were on high alert the entire time. During the bus ride to the jail, I heard stories told by the repeat offenders. They talked about gruesome murders and attacks that occurred in the jail that we were heading toward. The stories alone made my skin crawl. I wanted to jump out of the window as the old bus made its way to the gates. The sound of metal against metal grated my nerves. Chains linked together. Keys opening locks. It all haunted my thoughts during the day and my dreams late at night for years afterwards. I still wake up in a sweat from the nightmares. Jail is not for the faint of heart.

I sat in the cell with another gentleman who was

awaiting processing. His crime, first-degree murder. My cellmate was quiet and reserved, especially for someone accused of a malicious stabbing. He slept peacefully on the top bunk like he had no cares in the world. I spent those seventy-two hours wide-awake.

Jail is uncomfortable in every way. It is cold, the smell is deplorable and you don't have a say with whom or how many people are in there with you. Every right that you have is immediately taken away from you. You're not allowed to speak unless spoken to and you don't want to speak freely out of fear of the police or your cellmates responding in an unfavorable manner. Let me tell you now, that the struggle on the streets is better than a struggle behind bars. Life is too short to spend one day or night in a jail cell and I mean that with everything in me! That experience changed me for life.

I thought I was going to lose everything—my career, my properties in D.C. Godmom came to the police station, grabbed my wallet, and headed to the ATM. I was able to pay three thousand dollars to bail myself out of jail.

The first night home, I slept until noon the following day. That night I learned just how valuable a peaceful night's rest truly was. My family and friends called me with well wishes and prayers. Blessed to still have a network of supporters, even after all this time, they never questioned me, nor did they judge my situation. Mostly, we all behaved as if the situation didn't happen. Godmom continued to encourage and uplift me. She reminded me that my time wasn't over. It was just the beginning.

Thankfully, my attorney prevented me from having a mug shot taken. A disgraced politician was perfect news fodder. I avoided the utter humiliation of having my picture plastered on every news channel in the city. That was maybe the best thing about this situation. I didn't have to face as much public ridicule as I could have.

Everything weighed so heavily on my heart and spirit. I only wanted to make my mother and family proud. I had such lofty expectations for a great and successful life. I felt like the time I spent in jail erased my hard work.

I wasn't done. I had to work harder to prove it to myself. Life had knocked me down so many times before and I didn't wave the white flag. I refused to do so this time around. So, I served my seventy-two hours in jail and prepared myself for the possibility of facing five years in prison. Five years for a crime that didn't even make sense. It took me a while to accept what I did was a crime and to accept the potential punishment.

In my opinion, the right to vote shouldn't be limited. Every U.S. citizen should have the right to vote because no matter where they are, even if they are incarcerated, policies affect them. Furthermore, I believe it is unjust for someone convicted of a crime who serves their time, and yet not allowed to exercise a basic human right like voting. We could argue the points for and against this law for days, but I doubt this law will change any time soon. Thankfully, I avoided a long prison sentence, but that wasn't enough for me to feel victorious. My future was now at stake.

I have learned one thing about life: it does change rapidly. My advice is to be humble or prepare to be humbled. I have been down so many times before, but the possibility of spending five years in prison was the lowest I could conceive. Many years before my college education, I know I lived an unsavory life. I spent most of my free time doing accounting work for drug dealers and those who hung on the outskirts of society.

As the money man for most of the top guys in the organization, I counted more money than I could have ever imagined. I spent time counting money in abandoned houses that didn't have any furniture or running water, only a large table positioned in the kitchen with one light bulb hanging from the ceiling. I created businesses to clean money. I opened checking accounts for various businesses throughout the state of Mississippi. I was a professional long before I earned a college degree. The top cats in the game had that much faith in my abilities.

As I made money pickups and drop-offs, I fought ruminating thoughts that I would be arrested. The mere thought of prison terrified me and had my nerves on edge at times. I shrugged the thoughts off, telling myself all I had to do was be careful. The sheer coincidence of it all was not lost on me.

As hard as I worked to get out of the murkiness of the justice system, the deeper I sunk. I was a college-educated Black man who defeated many odds to get to where I stood. The fact that I ran for Congress at my age was enough to put my name in the record books, but here I was, facing prison time and a completely different kind of record.

There was no comforting, Johnnie Cochran to help me make the best decision for my future. My lawyer was a white woman who had been in the law business for years. She had advised me to plead guilty. "Plead guilty and avoid prison time," she said with an assured grin. I listened to the advice of my counsel and pled guilty to voter fraud.

I avoided prison time, but in 2014, I received a sentence of five years of probation. The thought of no prison time made the guilty plea more palatable. I did not realize how difficult this one thing would make my life. I, Cobby Mondale Williams, was now a convicted felon. "How can I bounce back from this?" I muttered to myself. In my mind, my ball had had its last bounce. There was no coming back from this point, at least not from my vantage point.

CHAPTER 9

THE BEST OF BOTH WORLDS

After the verdict, the school board learned of the case, which resulted in my termination. I could not return to substitute teaching. That same day, the hotel called me and said they were moving on to another candidate. My world was crumbling all around me. I had just signed the offer letter, but I could already see the impact my ignorance was having on my career. I was a convicted felon and no one wanted to hire me. My self-esteem had fizzled to the last drop. I could not take another demoralizing thing after being in court.

A police officer in the courthouse made me feel as if he had a personal alt against me and hated me for it. Officer Papet never seemed to relent on the verbal abuse while I was processed through the department the first time as well. Papet told me to "shut the fuck up" as often as he could, not letting me answer the questions I had been asked. He assured me that I would face the ire of him and his buddies every chance they got.

"If you're speeding, littering, or doing anything we find in violation of the law, you will be back here quicker than you can fathom." He whispered those angry words in my ear when he opened my cell for the final time. "And you won't enjoy it the second time around," he said with a wink.

I took the officer's words as a warning. I did not want any more trouble with the police department. All young, Black men should know how to avoid trouble with law enforcement. It is hard enough dealing with racism, stereotypes, and prejudices when you're an upstanding citizen. I had to get back into the world and be just that – a model citizen – but it seemed, despite my best efforts, Mississippi was not the place for me to excel.

The lack of job prospects and an overzealous, southern police department helped me make another incomprehensible decision. For the second time in my life, I packed my bags and loaded my car up for a one-way trip to Washington, D.C. I found myself back at the starting place from nearly fifteen years prior. This time, though, I was not running from the drug game. I was escaping the stigma of my ill-fated conviction.

It felt like everyone turned their back on me after that. No one wanted to rent an apartment to me or trust me to work in the bank. The "felon" persona changed my entire life. On the upside, it gave me a lot of time to reflect.

From my childhood entrepreneurial days, like selling pecans with my brother, to earning bachelor's and master's degrees, I had been defying the odds for decades now. I supposed there was truly nothing stopping me from rebuilding my life. Every time I felt down about my circumstances, I would state an affirmation. One of my favorites was, *"If I could do it once, surely I can do it again."* That affirmation was a powerful addition to my life. It helped me believe I could overcome negative energy and build a beautiful life.

As I was settling back in D.C., I called many of my prior contacts to see if they had any leads. I filled out application after application. I used headhunters and networking sources to find jobs, but they all seemingly led to a dead end. Every six-figure job I applied for, turned me down. I could not get beyond the background screening, let alone secure a job interview. That one question that appears on every job application haunted me: *Have you ever been convicted of a crime?* That question plagued my job searches and reminded me I had made a terrible mistake.

No, my mistake wasn't running for office or registering Melissa to vote. While those events led me to jail, they were not the catalyst. I underestimated how far someone would go to destroy the life of someone they disliked. My cousin, the one who I ran with for City Council, also received a conviction of voter fraud charges. Good ole Miss wasn't done with my family just yet. Someone wanted to make sure many of us never ran for office again. They went to great lengths for that.

I spent nights tossing and turning, wondering how things might be had I remained in D.C. I probably could have been at top levels; I at least could have been at GS-

15. The what-if scenarios sent me into a depressive spiral. I spent hours replaying what happened and beating myself up for doing one thing versus another. I thought about the ways my hard work had paid off the last time I was in D.C. I owned my first condominium and property in Baltimore that I had paid off. I had achieved some level of success, but I was emotionally scarred. It was dark and quiet within the four walls of my home. I never lived my life quietly, and it was hard to imagine a reserved version of myself. *"I have to get out of this,"* I told myself.

I wanted to serve the community and to encourage young people to shoot for the stars. To do that, I had to accept the past and the experiences that contributed to my character, personality, and accomplishments. I had to acknowledge my faults, as well. I am not proud of everything I've done, but I own my history. When I thought about other people with challenging backgrounds who have emerged successfully, I started to see that when you own your history, others may try to use it against you, but they cannot be the narrators of your story.

Thankfully, I found a way to rebuild my life through real estate. Real estate saved my livelihood after leaving Jackson. I rented out my property to earn monthly income. Airbnb® was a lifesaver! I owned property in D.C. near the RFK stadium in Northeast D.C. Over one hundred people stayed in my home and used my services. I am still friends with some of these folks and I am occasionally invited to visit their home country.

I could no longer afford the cost of maintaining my condo where I lived, so I sold it and moved to Baltimore, Maryland. I was fortunate to make enough money to pay cash for my home in Baltimore. The sense of security from that transition made an enormous difference in my cash flow and peace of mind.

Strangely, I began to feel grateful for the experiences I had while running for office. Although the end of my campaign was not ideal, I learned that I loved public service. I also learned that I loved teaching students. So, I brought my love for teaching and education to Maryland.

I spent a few years teaching in the Maryland public schools and then spent time in the District of Columbia Public Schools. It was eye-opening! Teaching in Mississippi was different. I felt accepted by the students because they knew I was from there. My students were eager to learn in the beginning. I did not have to work so hard to break the ice. In Baltimore, it seemed most of the children faced an uphill battle from birth. Several of my students had to navigate through a tough home environment to make it to school every day. Some were beaten by their parents. Others were homeless or sleeping in hostels. One student came to school describing the night the police officers kicked their front door open.

I tried to inspire them in the best way I knew how. They thought I was bragging, which led to believe that fighting me would somehow stop me from sharing my stories. My students had varying economic circumstances. While some kids did not have enough food to eat at home, yet others came to school flashing cash rolled into a tightwad. These students felt like they couldn't get anything out of school because they had everything they needed. Apparently, they had more than me! Unfortunately, their confidence in the cash in their pockets made them comfortable with disrupting my lessons regularly. I was experiencing spectacles from scenes in *Lean on Me*, *Dangerous Minds* and *Kindergarten Cop* all in the same week!

I knew being an educator meant facing certain obstacles with students, but I was angry about working a thankless job. Administration made me feel like I was not appreciated. Sometimes they made it difficult to go to work. I did my best to focus on the kids. I wanted my students to trust me, which is one reason I started sharing my experiences with them. I did not want to label them as "troubled youth" or "difficult" because a lot of their behavioral issues came from their life experiences.

I remembered taking my anger out on other students when I was in school. Like me, these kids had some emotions and they needed an avenue to express themselves. Fighting and acting out were just ways to get attention, albeit not the best ways. Nevertheless, there were plenty of pupils who were eager to learn. They gave me the confidence to continue my tenure at the school.

While others wouldn't listen to a word I said until they learned they could trust me.

I tried many ways to reach my students, but ultimately, my own reality provided the greatest connection. *How did I choose a better life path?* The answer to the question was exposure. If it were not for meeting Godmom and being exposed to a different way of thinking and living, I would still believe the lies my stepfather tried to implant. Since exposure helped me, I figured it would not hurt them. I found that my students learned better from exposure to different things, like art and science. I started taking them on field trips and one trip was to Maryland's Chesapeake Bay.

Although this was not my first teaching experience, it proved to be the most fruitful. The young minds were eager to discuss what they learned on their field trips. The look of wonder and awe on their faces was well worth it. I felt bad for the kids who wanted to learn but struggled because of the influence of the problematic students. Everything I did within my tenure of teaching felt as if it brought my life full circle. I felt like I was healing my own wounds by teaching and helping students feel heard and seen.

Teaching helped foster growth and maturity in me. I not only healed a few childhood wounds, but I also saw purpose in my struggle. While it was not always perfect, I learned a lot about myself and I could pass on practical lessons learned through my teaching. I did not realize that I carried resentment and anger throughout my life. There were days I found it challenging to set aside my emotions to handle a student with his or her own internal fury.

Therapy was extremely helpful to sorting out my feelings about my past and the impact on my present realities. I have had numerous discussions with my therapist about releasing anger and negativity. Somehow, I felt like little Cobby who was entering a new school with new kids. I especially grew frustrated when the kids didn't listen or got under my skin. I could feel the anger and frustration welling inside of me. I worked hard to be an efficient and caring teacher, but somehow it backfired on me. My soul felt drained and empty. Every morning, I willed myself to get up and show up for my students. Sadly, every evening when I returned home from work, I felt just like little Cobby, the ignored, misunderstood, and abused kid. I needed to talk to somebody about that.

Over time, I realized my blessings and learned how not to carry all the negative things said and done to me, but rather to find what has been positive outcomes or lessons learned. I learned methods to flip negative energy and use it as logs that fuel the fire burning under my feet and keep running toward my goals. It wasn't easy, but I tried.

I explored new ways to instruct my students there were better ways to handle situations. There were teachers with long tenure who helped me learn techniques for managing a classroom. They inspired me to encourage other young educators along the way. One teacher used comedy to engage his class. He made learning funny, which drew his students into his lessons. I wondered how I could share my experiences as a teacher in an authentic way, while maintaining control of the learning environment.

It took some time for my students to warm up to me. At first, some of them would say, "You sound like my father."

"Why?" I would ask.

"You sound like you care, but you're too serious."

After a while, we found better ways to communicate. Then, they got more comfortable and asked me more personal questions.

"Mr. Williams," one addressed me, "You got kids?"

"Yeah, how many kids you got?" Another chimed in.

"I don't have any children," I responded, sheepishly.

"Are you married?"

"Not yet," I sighed.

"Why not?"

"Mr. Williams," another changed the subject, "Why yo' voice sound so country? What kind of accent is that?" It was getting out of control. I tried to be as real as I could with the kids, but I found out the hard way that I couldn't be as real as I would have liked.

The conversation became heated and the students

started getting disrespectful and began cursing. As a teacher, there are some words you cannot use and things you can't say regardless of what the students say or do. Being "real" can get you in trouble on the professional side of life and that is what happened to me. That day, the students drove me to a limit and I lost it. I knew the minute I yelled (and it echoed throughout the entire school), it was time to leave Baltimore. The principal and two staff members came running down the hall at the sound of my booming voice. At least they showed some concern and started by asking if I was all right.

When students complained and recorded one of my speeches, and shared it with their parents and other teachers, the administration balked. It was time for a change and I was ready to go. I worked in Baltimore Public Schools as a Science and Social Studies Teacher for two years before I decided that that school district was not for me.

I continued with real estate until it seemed like God brought an answer to my unspoken prayers right to my doorstep. I was showing a house to a newlywed couple that had just returned from Ghana. The husband was so excited about his work in Ghana that he talked about it nonstop. He was a teacher and he rambled on and on about the students and how excited they were to learn English.

Something inside me jumped as I listened to his stories of his travels and teaching. *Hmm... travels and teaching?* I wondered to myself. My brain was running a mile a minute. I had to finish showing the house so I could go home and think about all I had just heard.

I searched my soul for answers. I spent days meditating, praying, and fasting. Finally, complete joy flooding every fiber of my being. I realized I was my happiest when I was traveling. I knew I wanted to be a trailblazer and wanted to do something different. I still really loved teaching, too. The thought of bringing those two worlds together was exhilarating! I threw caution to the wind and decided to use my education experience and my love for travel to become an international teacher.

I applied to several different programs online. I worked hard, trying to find the best fit. I wanted to work for an organization that represented me fairly and treated me well; especially since I would live overseas. I can admit that I was skeptical. Based on how Black people are treated in America, I was apprehensive as I considered moving to another country. Who wouldn't be? Before I knew it eight different companies offered me a job. This was the first time in a long time where I felt needed. It was the self-esteem boost I so desperately needed. My life was not over after all.

CHAPTER 10

ANOTHER NEW BEGINNING

After two years of paperwork, background checks and approvals, I finally had everything I needed to begin life in China. Just weeks before I boarded my plane, I rented out my apartment, sold my car and donated many of my clothes and shoes. My family was not surprised about my move at all. They knew how much I loved traveling abroad. After all the preparation and my business was in order, I was ready for my new adventure.

As the plane descended to Guiyang airport, I saw patterns of luscious green mountains, paved roads, valleys, and condensed cities. I had lived in many places, but China was very new and different for me. I found a studio apartment that, by Chinese living standards, was large. The only thing that shocked me was the design of the bathroom. Everything seemed to fit inside the shower. The toilet, sink, and the shower stall had one large drain in the center. The appliances were a tad smaller than conventional American sizes, but everything was sleek and shiny in my new home. The whole place was modern – from the vent fan hanging over the stove down to the coffee maker that had a digital touch screen.

My apartment was on the twenty-fifth floor of the Bai Yun Shan about six miles from the Interlinga International School. This place was called other names that I had to remember to get a taxicab home, like "White Cloud Mountain." After it rained, light clouds seemed to hover around the peak like soft, cotton candy. I could see the mountain each morning when I opened the blinds to my bedroom and walked onto my balcony. Pure joy flooded my soul each day I gazed at the beautiful landscape. This mountain was "My Rock," I called it, as it reminded me of Psalm 18:2 (NIV), *"The Lord is my rock, my fortress, and my deliverer; my God is my rock, in whom I take refuge, my shield and the horn of my salvation, my stronghold."* It was a place of overwhelming peace.

The way the sun shone upon me and the towering height of mountains made me realize each morning that I was not "in Kansas anymore." The apartment buildings were like skyscrapers built to accommodate the large population of over eight million within the area. While everything was breathtaking, one drawback was that the walls had no insulation. During the winter months, primarily November through December, I had to utilize heating blankets and multiple heaters to keep warm.

Every day as I left my apartment and headed toward the elevator, I was greeted by a seventy-year-old couple, and their grandbaby greeted me. Mr. and Mrs. Chen spoke to me in Mandarin while smiling from ear to ear. The genuine greeting warmed my heart daily. The Chen's reminded me of my grandparents every time I saw them together. It was something about their closeness that reminded me of a certain bond that felt all too familiar.

On the main floor of the building there were five to ten senior citizens sitting at tables playing board games. I was not interested in knowing what they were playing during the first few months. After all, I was just learning to speak the language. When I finally decided to speak to them, I wanted to make a good first impression. There were many private tutors teaching Mandarin so I took advantage of their services. I took pictures of the notes from my tutor and kept a journal as well. My students also helped me learn the fundamentals of the language, too. One day at the game tables, a man invited me to see what all the excitement was about. I suppose curiosity got the best of us all. I learned they were playing Wei Qi (Go). There were other board games, but this game was one of the world's oldest games and was extremely popular in China.

Go reminded me of how my family and friends played Spades. Individuals were yelling and screaming at each other if they made mistakes, which was soon followed by outbursts of laughter. By watching the men playing Go, I learned how similar people are even though we have different ethnicities.

I would commute to work by bus or taxi. Bus rides in Guiyang were crazy. Some days, the bus would be half empty, and other days we were packed like sardines. Although taxis were much more comfortable, the challenge was communicating with the taxi driver where I needed to go. I had to spell the location and school's name on paper to show the driver.

It took a while to get used to people staring at me and stopping me to take pictures. It wasn't because they thought I was a celebrity. It was because they had never seen a Black man in person. I was a phenomenon to them! Shop owners would stop serving others when I walked inside their stores, just to take a picture with me to advertise their business. Parents dropped babies in my arms and pulled out their cameras. I smiled politely when I walked into a public place and suddenly found myself the center of attention. I was pleasantly surprised at the number of new friends I met this way. This reaction to a Black man outside of America was refreshing. They were not afraid of me, but rather I intrigued them. They didn't treat me like a second-class citizen either. This certainly helped with my anxieties about getting acclimated to a strange place, but it did not help everything.

Street food was my biggest weakness and it often resulted in discomfort. I indulged in Jianbing (crepes), Rou Jia Mo (hamburgers), Jiaozi (a dumpling filled with vegetables or your choice of meat) and pork chops with rice cakes. Almost all food China had to offer, but I was often sick as a dog from the constant eating out. Several times I felt like the world was closing in on my stomach. Each time it lasted for a few days before I was back to normal again. When it was the worst, I ended up in the hospital. This happened three times and I was extremely uncomfortable because most of the hospitals were very unsanitary. The equipment used by the staff was outdated and appeared rusted. The floors and beds looked as though they had not been cleaned in months or even years. Even still, all of that still didn't stop me from trying new foods.

I had only been at Interlingua School for two months and my birthday was approaching at the end of July. I worked with an amazing group of people while teaching in China. There was Paul from Texas and Chris from Scotland. The locals from various parts of China were Adinah, Mang, Irian, Irene, Den a Yi, Cathy, and Sara. They wanted to know everything about me and I enjoyed sharing about myself. I loved just being Cobby. I didn't have to be perfect or conform to anyone's personal rules. I did not have to conform to an expected persona nor did I have to defend my unconventional choices. I didn't feel like eyes were on me everywhere I went. In China, I finally found Cobby.

Only July 31st, the staff shocked me with a surprise birthday party. At that point, I only had three birthday parties in my life so their gesture was memorable. Being the emotional person I am, this brought tears to my eyes. It reminded me of the immense hospitality I experienced in my other travels, particularly Costa Rica and Ethiopia. In China, they treated me like family and I believed that being there was the culmination of my hard work. Teaching students English, preparing their lesson plans, and helping them become more engaged was a joy. I learned more from the students of Guiyang than I could have ever imagined.

During my nine-month tenure, the school grew, and I learned most of my students by name. Some Chinese people have many names, of which I struggled to pronounce. It worked it my favor that they were eager to have an American name to simplify their own. I had the pleasure of working with some of the parents to help adapt the names of some of my favorite students. To their delight, I was able to come up with American names that suited them just nicely. I recall naming some of them: Mia, Thomas, Jerry, Bob, Nicole, Nate, and Susie were some of my favorite students.

My excitement grew with each passing minute of greeting them in the mornings. Those smiling, energetic, cheerful little beings gave a part of me hope of having my own children one day. They loved school. Every day there was a room full of twenty-five students, all eager to learn. It was a different atmosphere. It felt wonderful to know the students valued what I was teaching. No one challenged me or tried to be the class clown. They all sat quietly and intently listening to my every word. These children did not play about their education! The school day began at 7:30 a.m., concluding around 5:00 p.m. The difference between these students and the ones I left in

Baltimore was startling and damn near alarming.

In the States, I lost count of the times I received a tongue lashing for disciplining a child. Some of the parents in Baltimore were worse than the children. Parents make the difference just as much as the teachers. In China, the parents respected teachers, and they made sure their children showed respect. In my observation, they placed a higher value on education as a culture than I than parents in the U.S. After nursing my childhood wounds and dealing with the pain that came along with teaching in Baltimore, China was a breath of fresh air. It was absolutely refreshing in every way.

One of the largest German hotels in Guiyang was across the street from the school. While dining at the coffee shop, thoughts of my childhood and family crossed my mind. Tears of joy rolled down my cheeks as I realized I was experiencing the result of another tenacious, yet bold, move to be different. Who would have thought I would leave Mississippi and find myself in such a faraway land? I was a dreamer, but even I didn't see this in my future. I was grateful. Still there were times when I missed home. I also thought I might be missing something at home. I still didn't have the romantic relationship I wanted and seeing those children reminded me that I did not have that yet.

To take my mind off things, I would venture out to see some of China's most beautiful places when school wasn't open. One place I had the pleasure of visiting was

Dali China, a city in China's southwestern Yunnan province, on the shores of Erhai Lake. It was about four hours from where I lived by ground transportation and two hours by flight. Sure, I had visited neighboring small cities, but Dali was different.

In Dali, many of the Buddhist sights captivated me. Dali had pagodas, grottoes, temples, and Buddhists' mountains. The sculptures and paintings were so detailed and colorful. Some were so old that I wondered how long they had been there. I walked through villages and listened to music. It was often opera. Those moments I will treasure for life. My life almost ended twice and I would have missed all of this. It is remarkable how being transported across the world can make you understand how precious life is. The experiences I had in China helped me to come to grips with how blessed I truly was.

When I left Mississippi the last time, I felt like a cloud of disappointment was permanently over my life. Teaching international students within their home country was so fulfilling that it helped heal some of the wounds that Mississippi caused. It reminded me that no matter what happened to me, I was still Cobby. I was still a public servant, still a person who wanted to give back and still determined to succeed.

Back at the school, the staff and I would talk about other places in the country I should visit during our upcoming breaks, but I had other countries on my mind, particularly African countries, like Ghana, and vacation time was approaching for the entire country. The Chinese citizens were preparing to celebrate Chinese New Year. Celebrations start sometime between January and February. At the beginning of 2020, I was teaching my students about the Chinese Zodiac, with each year of a twelve-year cycle related to an animal sign. The year 2020 was the year of the rat. They were learning the English words for all the other animals in the zodiac. The students thought it was fun and enjoyed drawing and coloring the animal that represented them.

The holiday vacation began a few days after our lesson. I booked my ticket for Beijing to get my visa for Ghana. The Ghanaian embassy walked me through the process with ease. While I waited two days for my visa, I received my immunizations and toured Beijing to the fullest. I visited government institutions and historic museums, but I was most eager to see the Great Wall of China. I remembered that the politician I admired as a child in Jackson had a picture of it on the wall in his office. Unfortunately, I did not make it. "I'll just do it on my way back to China from Ghana," I said to myself aloud.

A few days after we celebrated the Chinese New Year, I flew to Ghana. The name Ghana means "warrior," and that is exactly how I felt when I stepped off the plane in Accra. I felt like a Warrior King! The sudden wave of power emanating from the ground in Ghana was mesmerizing. The Dome Chateau Bed and

Breakfast was about an hour away from the airport and very nice – better than I expected. The grand staircase was captivating as I entered the lobby. Outside on the rooftop, the views of the city and the ocean were breathtaking.

I was curious and could not wait to learn as much as I could about the country. What surprised me most was that Ghana ranks as one of the best education systems in Africa and even though it does not rank high economically, this doesn't stop students from walking to school or attending classes barefoot because they can't afford shoes. Even when it is the hardest thing to do, I watched children set aside hunger and lack to learn.

This saddened me when I compared my time in Ghana to that of Baltimore. Unlike in China, these children reminded me of myself and my Baltimore students. They looked like me. We shared the same skin complexion. I wished I could have taken the experience back to Baltimore to say to the students there, "See? This is how blessed these kids feel to learn. Why don't you feel this blessed? Why do you take your education for granted when these kids know the value of it all?" I would have asked them to re-evaluate their mindset about going to school. I knew in my heart that nothing would change their minds. The kids in Baltimore and Jackson lived privileged lives compared to the children I met in Ghana. They just didn't know it.

During my visit to a school in Ghana, I was greeted

with warmth and open arms. The simple infrastructure of cement floors and a tin roof was devoid of modern amenities like shiny walls or iPads. Yet, I found a profound beauty in the hearts of the students and their unwavering determination to excel. Despite the absence of luxuries such as heating or cooling systems, the radiant smiles on the faces of the children illuminated the environment with hospitality and genuine warmth. Their liveliness about my presence filled me with joy and deeply touched my heart. The experience profoundly impacted my perspective of life and the privilege of education.

The children honored me with a traditional dance performance of the Ghanaian culture. While they prepared for the celebration, I took the opportunity to explore the campus, visiting each classroom and connecting with the students. Though the ethnic groups of Ghana have many traditional dances, the kids put on a spirited show of five rhythmic numbers, treating me to a kpalongo dance where they sang and danced with joy to drums. They also performed the Agbadza, Adowa, Bambaya, and Kpatsa dances. They gave me goosebumps and pushed me to move to the rhythm almost uncontrollably. After the celebration ended, I had dinner with the children. I had never felt so humbled. These children appeared to be at their happiest in the world as if they had never missed a meal in their lives whereas back home, I attributed some of my students' poor behavior to a lack of food and home structure. I learned that the environment alone does not make the kid. It is possible to have dire circumstances and still smile, dance and sing.

Traveling through Ghana was not only an educational experience; it was also an emotional one. Memories of my visit to the *Door of No Return* in Elmina cause my eyes to well up to this day and they stir something in my spirit. It was a hub of slave trading in Ghana. Over the door there is a brass plaque that reads "Door of No Return." That door was the last door that captive Africans went through before they boarded ships and were sold as slaves.

I lost my composure standing in front of that door. The tour guide stood back and patted me on the shoulder as emotions took over. I thanked him after we left the site and he waved his hand, casually, as if he expected my reaction. He must have seen similar reactions a thousand times. I stood and watched the waves crash against the shore, visualizing the agony my people endured. I imagined the ancestors journeying through this door and being strong enough to survive the hell they faced. I considered the hardships and demoralization they suffered just so I could be me.

Travel changes you in immeasurable ways. China and Ghana matured me. In China, I learned to be open minded and not to be afraid to utilize all my skills. I suppose it was there I also learned not to be fearful of letting my guard down – to trust people and allow them to earn my trust. Whereas Ghana, opened my eyes to how strong my people truly were and how much we endured as a people. We did not come from the bottom. We were kings and queens, with great wealth, stolen from our homes, and sent to a foreign land to work for free. The miracle is that I can run for Congress in the same country where my ancestors worked as slaves. Ghana reminded me of the sheer power in our bloodlines. I was eager to continue my travels and yet I missed home. Suddenly, not only my life changed, but everyone around me.

CHAPTER 11

THE LONGEST YEAR OF MY LIFE

In the last few days of my trip, I reviewed my Ghana excursion itinerary. I experienced nightlife at the Sky Bar and Movenpick Hotel. In Accra, I toured Kwame Nkrumah Center, Art Center, Black Star Square, Jamestown and Makola Market. We went on the Senchi Boat Ride and visited the Akosombo Dam. Of course, the Ghana School System was a highlight for me because of the children. I started getting excited to get back to my students in China and tell them what I had seen and learned, but then, I turned on the television.

The news outlets had started speaking about some kind of virus that started in Wuhan, which is about five hours from where I lived. It wasn't close per se, but it was close enough for me to be alarmed.

"What in the world is going on?" I asked my boss when I finally had the chance to speak with her.

"Things will get better after a few weeks. Just return when it does," my boss responded, positively. *Return when it does?* I sort of expected that from her. She was all about business. How could I blame her?

"I would love to get back to the students and the school," I responded, checking my phone for other details. My flight back to China was cancelled! I glanced at the top of my excursion itinerary, which clearly stated, "Itinerary is subject to change and/or substitution including places and times." I rolled my eyes. *They couldn't have prepared for this!* My boss didn't know that my flight back to China was canceled so she tried to remain positive. We ended the conversation somewhat upbeat, but I panicked.

I woke up on January 30, 2020, to a very strange message. The World Health Organization had declared COVID-19 an international health emergency. China had shutdown Wuhan. Businesses were closed and people were quarantined to their homes. Thank God for WeChat! I used the app to communicate with my colleagues back in China. They were devastated and worried.

First Kobe Bryant, now this? I was still trying to grapple with the death of an icon along with all the other people in the world who admired him. *What am I going to do about my students, my apartment, and my job?* My hard work and things I've accumulated over the months and years were now in jeopardy back in China. Thoughts of how I would manage my finances were hanging over my head. I started looking at pictures of my students on my phone. My heart dropped. All the times shared, videos, parties, and field trips and more memories started weighing heavily on my heart. Tears began rolling down my face. *What am I going to do now?*

By February 2nd, flights from China to the US were

being restricted. My reasonable fears were quickly turning into terror. The more I listened to the news and tried to get more information, it seemed the less I knew. As airports were closing, I was in a devastating situation. I needed to fly back to China to collect my belongings and then return home to DC. However, that was looking more and more impossible. China was the epicenter of the virus and its cities began to shut down one by one.

The conversations with my colleagues were limited, but intense. They spoke about being in survival mode and staying safe, whatever that meant. It was too new for us all to really grasp what was going on. I could hear the fear in their voices.

"We'll get through this together," I would say, optimistically. There was often silence on the other end of the phone after that. It seemed nothing I said gave them any sense of hope or comfort.

Meanwhile, on television, the news stories described everyone in major Chinese cities were placed on "house arrest" and was limited to moving about in the community. Everyone had to be in their homes by a certain time of night. Delivery was the only way people could get food. Only caregivers or hospital employees could move about somewhat freely. Even more alarming was the number of people dying increasing by the second.

WeChat gave me access to some of the parents and I had the opportunity to speak with many students, who were in good spirits. That made me smile... for a week!

After that, the parents weren't saying anything anymore. It was like a switch was turned off and everything went silent. China was limiting their communications with the world!

About three weeks into the pandemic, it seemed everyone in my circle barely talked on social media. My landlord said they couldn't move or go anywhere. Abruptly, after multiple emails, texts, and calls, she stopped responding. WeChat went silent. At this point, the shit hit the fan. Reality hit that I was stuck in Ghana and China had a door of no return!

My life in China was over. I learned that everyone there stopped communicating with me because they had strict lockdown on communications outside of China. Any form of communication was being monitored and negative communications were strictly prohibited. They were told that anyone who contracts the virus had to report to the hospital immediately. Quarantining was all based on the severity of symptoms. Some people could be in complete isolation for two to three weeks. They forced people to stay home to limit the exposure. My wardrobe was down to three pairs of shorts, five T-shirts, two pairs of shoes. My apartment and all my belongings became less and less important.

As the news outlets began sharing that the virus had reached the United States, I called back home to check with friends and family about what was going home. I thought, "Maybe I have to leave Ghana and go back to

D.C." I got mixed messages depending upon who I spoke with and where they lived. Some were panicking. Some said nothing was happening in their area. New York, however, seemed to be in the same situation as China and body bags were piling up.

"We are shutting down states and wearing masks," one friend said.

"The government is getting ready to give us a vaccine," said another.

"We have to get vaccinated in order to work!" my brother yelled. It was an emotional roller coaster ride. Ironically, it was a comedy show talking with my brothers and sister. They weren't taking this seriously. Some thought it was a conspiracy. All I knew was, I didn't have a home to go to and I had to figure out how I was going to work, eat and sleep while the world figured out how to remain healthy.

Even though I was eager to return to the United States, I could rest assured that I would get out of the situation just fine. I had been moving at a rapid speed for years. Maybe this was my time to be still and rest. I tried my best not to panic. Instead, I kept my family posted of my situation using Instagram. It helped calm their fears and it gave me something to do.

Just like the saying goes, everything happens for a reason. I used that time to do some soul searching. Events of my life flashed before me. God has kept His hand on me through missteps at work, a challenging political experience, and grappling with my own education. I even thought about the abuse I endured from my childhood. I had already survived a volatile life. I remembered the nights I spent in sketchy areas, counting thousands of dollars for dangerous dealers. The gun violence I survived and the car accidents that left me damaged, but alive. That was when it hit me. I am still here.

There must be something much greater than what I had already done. God has spared my life for something big. I had survived so much in my life. Surely, I could survive this, I thought. I'm not saying I was as cool as a cucumber, but I didn't completely lose myself.

After weeks of sitting around and moping, I decided to get out of my room at the Dome Chateau and begin looking for work. I went back to some of the local schools I had visited earlier in the year when I first arrived. My tour guide introduced me to each of the schools' leaders and that's when the door of opportunity opened. Mastab Prepatory School welcomed me like family. It wasn't far from my hotel either.

I was more than grateful for this opportunity because, after several months of being stuck in Ghana, I learned that my school in China had closed, seemingly indefinitely. I was surprised that I wasn't deported, but then again, the U.S. had closed many international airports, too. I couldn't go back to China and I couldn't go home. I decided to make the best of my time in Ghana and let the chips fall where they may.

I chose to visit Togo, which was just east of Ghana, to clear my head and figure out my next move. Togo was one of the most beautiful places I had ever visited. It was interesting to hear people speaking French in Western Africa. Its place on the Gulf of New Guinea made the beaches pristine. There were a lot of tourists there even at that time.

More beautiful than the country of Togo are the hearts of the people who live there. Many of the locals greeted me with warm smiles and kind words. No matter where I went, people asked where I was from and if they could take a picture with me. Many people invited me to their homes. I felt like family more in Togo than in many places back in the United States. I felt like a king as we feasted on delicious delicacies like Fufu and vegetable stew when we gathered.

I spent a few hours working with a kind lady who showed me how to knead the dough for Fufu. I met people from different walks of life, from educators to businessmen to farmers. I fondly remember the taste of Tchoukoutou. It is a local beer with an acquired taste that I yearn for from time to time even now.

When I returned to Ghana, I was happy to be with my students. Considering the poverty, I became acutely aware of my surroundings there, and yet, I felt very safe and secure. I became more supportive of the people of Ghana. Despite the emotional trauma within me, I was so grateful to have a community that was filled with love as

I started this new work at the prep school. It was as if I didn't miss a beat. The kids were excited and I didn't feel trapped anymore.

I believed that God had brought me to a place where I could stand still and see His salvation. I felt I truly understood the importance of cherishing life. Taking care of yourself in all ways (physically, mentally, emotionally, spiritually) is what matters. Life had taught me that worrying would only get me closer to death's door, a door I didn't want to go through too soon.

I'm glad I'm alive to say that. If my life had ended when I was sixteen, I would have missed so many wonderful opportunities. I would have missed the kindheartedness of people from all over the world. I would have missed maturing from observing old men and young minds. These were my reflections as I was on my way back from Togo.

"I got your back, Cobby," my uncle said, reassuringly. Before I knew it, he purchased a one-way plane ticket to Dulles International Airport. I'll never forget that; I was sitting in the kitchen of my temporary home. I felt so relieved. I had so much on my mind – the kids back in China, my apartment there and even my new students. *Is this deadly disease on its way to Africa?*

I closed my eyes, inhaled, and let out a deep breath. Again, I reflected on my life in Jackson. *If I can make it through that, I can get through this!* I spent an entire year in Ghana. Though it was a short-lived, it was the longest year of my life and memories of its lessons will not soon be forgotten.